EVERYTHING THAI
TOP 10'S OF THAILAND

The Guide of Highlights

To
Auntie Pat

Happy Reading

B. Sorin Sart

Copyright

Title book: Everything Thai Top 10's Of Thailand

Author book: Ben Sonimsart / Lacey

CONTENTS

PREFACE

ABOUT THE AUTHOR

Hi. My name is Ben Sonimsart and I am half Thai and half English. I first travelled to Thailand at the age of 4 years old in 1991. Since then, I have been fortunate enough to visit Thailand multiple times and experience the country both as a tourist and a local. I wrote this book to help me share my knowledge and experiences with you. The ultimate goal is to provide you with top tips, advice, and great ideas which will help you make the very best out of your visit to Thailand.

ABOUT THE BOOK

By using a combination of my own personal experiences and advice from my Thai family and other travellers, I have developed a book to showcase the top 10 experiences and subjects which people are most interested in when it comes to visiting Thailand. In each of the chapters, I recommend the top 10 options for each area of interest. Again, this is done using a mix of my own personal experiences and advice from my Thai family & other travellers. The book covers everything from the most popular destinations and experiences to the much lesser known. Each chapter presents options for Central, Southern and Northern Thailand.The book was never intended to be a full blown guide book with overwhelming amounts of information. Instead, it is user friendly, easy to navigate, and will save the reader months of research. Although very informative, it is still designed to be simple and straight to the point. High quality photos have been used to better aid you in your research. Its is also important to note that none of the top 10 selections have been choosen in a particaulr order.

CHAPTER 1 TOP 10 TEMPLES

1) Grand Palace – Bangkok

The Grand Palace is not technically a temple, but within its grounds is the Temple of the Emerald Buddha (Wat Phra kaew). Recognized as one of the most iconic and important temples and Buddha statues in Thailand, the famous Emerald Buddha statue was actually carved from a single block of jade. The best part of visiting this temple is that you get to enjoy the Grand Palace grounds and several other buildings on the same visit.

Photo Credit: Travel Mania /shutterstock.com

Everywhere you look, your eyes will be met with well-planned landscaping, beautiful artworks, intricate designs, and stunningly detailed architecture. Originally built in 1782, the Grand Palace was used by the Royal family until the turn of the 20th century. It was then used by government organisations and for ceremonies of high importance. The character and charm of the palace have never been lost due to the great standard of maintenance and preservation techniques used. Another great thing about visiting the Grand palace is its location. It is close to Wat Po and Wat Arun, allowing a visit to all three in one day. Each temple is very different yet spectacular. The Jounrney between them allows for refreshing breaks in between.

Location: Na Phra Lan Road, Grand Palace, Phranakorn, Bangkok 10200. **Opening times:** 08.30 -15.30 **Entrance Fee:** Yes

2) Wat Pho – Bangkok

Believed to be founded in the 16th century and restored in 1801 under King Rama I, Wat Pho is home to the famous giant golden reclining Buddha, which is approximately 150 feet long (one of the largest in the world). It is also well known for being the official home for the education and teachings of the traditional Thai massage. Spread over 8 hectares, it is normally a little less crowded than the Grand Palace. Wat Pho has plenty to explore, from small to large colourful Chedis spread around the complex and including the largest collection of Buddha images in Thailand.

Photo Credit Attem /shutterstock.com

Being the official school of the traditional Thai massage, you can take the opportunity to break up your visit and indulge in a true Thai massage. The prices are slightly more here, but are worth every extra baht for a truly authentic experience. Literally walking distance from the Grand Palace and with Wat Arun only a short boat ride over the Chao Phraya River, the location of Wat Pho makes for easy access to two of Thailand's other famous temples.

Location: Maharat Road, on the river side and south of the Grand Palace
Opening times: 08.30 – 17.00
Entrance Fee: Yes

3) Wat Arun – Bangkok

Just off the banks of the Chao river sits the majestic Wat Arun (Chaeng)! Its name translates to the temple of dawn, however the name actually originates from the Indian God Aruna. This temple is quite different in comparison to others you will see in Bangkok. Standing at just over 70 metres tall, its main structure is made out of formed concrete, which has been decorated in detailed and elaborate patterns with the use of Chinese porcelain and colour stained glass. This Temple offers an opportunity to climb parts of it, which can be accessed by steps and purpose-made platforms to give you additional views and amazing photo opportunities. The temple's breathtaking beauty is best appreciated when the sun is low, particularly at sunrise and sunset.

Photo credit Zanettpix /shutterstock.com

The story of Wat Arun is quite interesting. It is said to be first envisioned by King Taksin in 1768. After his battle with the Burmese in Ayutthaya, he escaped and arrived at the temple grounds just after dawn was breaking. He then went on to rename and renovate it to what we now know as Wat Arun. It is intended to be an architectural and symbolic representation of Mount Meru, which in Buddhism and Hinduism is believed to be the centre of the world, universe, and the natural habitat of both spirits and Gods.

Location: Arun Amarin Road, next to the Chao Phraya River, opposite to Wat Pho.
Opening Times 07.30 - 17.30 Entrance Fee: Yes

4) Wat Rong Khun - Chiang Rai

Also known as the White Temple, Wat Rong Khun has to be one of Thailand's most unique and unconventional temples. Designed by Chalermchai Kositpipat, a locally born visual artist and painter, the temple features traditional Buddhist symbolism. Paired with his own interpretations, he created a temple that tells stories and conveys important messages at every twist and turn. Be sure to bring your sunglasses as bright white colours have been used instead of the common gold (to demonstrate pureness). Many of the designs include mirrors that have been delicately placed and incorporated into the architecture.

Photo credit: Shuttertong /shutterstock.com

It truly is a special and unique temple which presents so many photo opportunities and surprises along the way. It has even been said to be home to one of Thailand's most beautiful Temple restrooms (yes, you read that right)! From trees that have been created initially from wishes written by visitors on silver plates to the bridge you must cross that spans over a sea of hands reaching up from the depths of hell. You will encounter sculptures of mythical creatures and paintings of modern icons used to tell stories of Buddha himself! The mixture of traditional architecture along with its artistic modern twist will keep you thinking and interested throughout your visit.

Location: Lahaul-Spiti, Pa O Don Chai Subdistrict, Chiang Rai.
Opening Hours: 06.30 – 18.00 daily (temple); 08:00 – 17:30 Mon-Fri (museum of paintings) Entrance Fee: Yes

5) Sanctuary of Truth – Pattaya

Technically, this isn't a temple but a representation of many Asian faiths and religions, including ancient mythology. The Sanctuary of Truth is built out of teak wood, which is hand carved and pieced together without the use of a single nail. Construction on this mesmerising temple-like structure commenced in 1981 and is said to still be in construction. The idea for the Sanctuary of Truth was created by Thai millionaire, Lek Vinyaphant, who wanted to revive long lost skills such as hewn wood work. His aim was to tell an ongoing story of goodness and achievement drawn from all religion by humans.

Photo Credit Mary Joy Barong/shutterstock.com

The architecture, intricate details, the message, the forward thinking, and the skills used to create the Sanctuary of Truth are a true credit to Thailand's remarkable craftsmanship. Don't worry if you are not overly religious as a visit here will still be worth it. Just walking through the structure, which is literally carved out with thousands of sculptures, is amazing in itself. Also, with Thailand being Thailand, there are a few unexpected attractions within the grounds such as, theatrical sword fighting displays and a small shooting range. Finally, its idyllic location of being right by the beach makes for a great visit.

Location: 206/2 Moo5, Pattaya-Naklua Road Soi 12, Naklua
Opening times: 08:00 - 17:00 Entrance Fee: Yes

6) Wat Tha Sung - Uthai Thani

Also known as the Glass temple, this temple was originally constructed in the Ayutthaya period. Although there are little hints of glistening mirrors included in the exterior design of the roof, looking in from the outside it's hard to imagine what awaits you inside this temple. Once you enter the main hall, you will be met with the most elaborate of interior designs. With the use of shiny glass and mirrors, everything from walls to columns, and even the ceiling, has been decorated to reflect light across all areas. Although this sounds a little bit too much, it really is a sight to be seen.

Photo Credit defpicture/shutterstock.com

The temple is also home to the replica Buddha statute, Phra Phuttha Chinnarat, which is said to be one of the most beautiful in Thailand. The grounds to this temple include large well-kept areas to stroll along whilst relaxing on your visit and pavilions which accommodate meditation. Across the road is "The Golden Castle" (Prasat Thong-kam). Although not a temple, it is well worth including as part of your visit as it has a real royal feel to it. Other activities here include feeding of the fish in the nearby river as a way of merit. You can also take boat tours along the river, all of which are very reasonably priced.

Location: Mu 2, Tambon Nam Sum, Amphoe Mueang, Uthai Thani
Opening times: 09.00 - 16.00
Entrance Fee: Yes

7) Wat Mahathat – Ayutthaya

Step back in time with a visit to Wat Mahathat. Located in Ayutthaya, the old capital of Thailand. It is thought that this once royal Buddhist temple was built in the 14th century and stood until 1767, when Ayutthaya was invaded and over run by the Burmese, destroying much of the city and the temple. In the 1950s, the department of fine arts started restoration works to the temple and surrounding areas, and have done a great job so far. By keeping as much of the original buildings and using as much of the original material as possible, it has ensured that Wat Mahathat and its surrounding grounds have kept their true character and ancient feel.

Photo Credit vectorx2263/shutterstock.com

Many of the damaged buildings have been left as they once stood all those years ago. It is also home to the iconic and famous Buddha's head entwined in the roots of a tree. It is so famous and sacred to the Thais that there is actually a guard stationed here at all times. All in all, if you are a fan of history and want to see some of Thailand's most ancient and original temples, this is the place to go.

Location: Ayutthaya Historical Park | Pratuchai, Phra Nakhon Si, Ayutthaya 13000.
Opening times: 08.30 – 17.00
Entrance Fee: Yes

8) Phraya Nakhon Cave - Hao Sam Roi Yot National Park

A visit here is as much about the journey to your destination as it is the destination itself. The main pavilion in the cave was built at the end of the 19th century, with smaller shrines dotted around under smaller alcoves of the main cave. This location was very popular with the past kings of Thailand. To get to the Phraya Nakhon cave, the easiest route is by taking a boat from the village of Bang Pu to Laem Sala beach. The beach itself is clean and usually fairly quiet. Further up from the beach, you can find a rural restaurant to visit, either before or after your hike to the Phraya Nakhon cave.

Photo Credit S-F/shutterstock.com

The climb up is appox 430 metres, and the humidity can be quite intense at times. However, do not let this put you off! You are in Hao Sam Roi national park, and with that comes many opportunities to experience some amazing nature and wildlife. You can find lizards, colourful butterflies and, if you're lucky, the dusty leaf monkey, which can only be found in Thailand, Myanmar, and Malaysia. There are also many resting spots along the rocky route, including a half way view point, which looks out over the surrounding sea and smaller islands. Once you arrive at the opening to the cave, be prepared to be mesmerised.

Location: Hao Sam Roi Yot National Park.
Opening times: 08.30 -15.30
Entrance Fee: Yes

9) Tiger Cave Temple (Wat Tham Suea) - Krabi

Despite the temple's name, this temple has no real tigers. It was given its name due the Tiger foot prints which can be found in one of the temple's caves. The name also comes from the fact that Monks claim the tigers were still using the caves up until the 1970s, at the same time as the monks. A visit here is best suited to active and adventurous travellers. It's a 1237 step hike up this small mountain to reach the top, and its main attraction. You will be instantly rewarded with sweeping 360° views of the surrounding landscapes, which include mountains, rain forests and the Andaman sea.

Photo Credit Decha kiatlatchanon /shutterstock.com

The temple is still used by practicing monks which actually live in the maze of caves at the bottom of the hill. Most of the caves have been converted into temple and worship areas. They are elaborately decorated with many golden Buddha statues and marble floors, just like you would find in a typical Thai Temple. The Monks who reside here practice a branch of Buddhism called Vipassana, focusing mainly on mediation.

TOP TIP: Visit early morning to beat the heat, avoid the crowds and the monkeys.

Location: Krabi Noi, Mueang Krabi District, Krabi 81000
Opening Times: Always open
Entrance Fee: No – but small donations to support the temple are always welcome.

10) Wat Tham Pha Plong -Chiang Dao

This temple is in no way as grand or elaborate as many of the other temples mentioned, but it is easily the one of the most peaceful and is also full of charm. Located amongst the mountains and evergreen forests, it is slightly off the beaten path and a great alternative to Tiger Temple or the Phraya Nakhon Cave. You get to be away from it all, take in great views and nature as well as experience an authentic Thai temple without the crowds. From the bottom of Wat Tham Pha Plong, it is a comfortable walk up 500 well built steps. Compared to Tiger temple, which is over double that amount. The temple was founded by Abbot Luang Pu Sim in 1967; and he remained there until his death in 1992. He was and still is a highly revered monk throughout Thailand.

Photo Credit saiko3p/shutterstock.com

TOP TIP: Don't forget to check out the Top 10 tips chapter, which covers advice for visiting temples.

Location: 139 5 Tambon Chiang Dao, Amphoe Chiang Dao
Opening Times: Always open
Entrance Fee: No – but small donations to support the temple are always welcome.

CHAPTER 2 TOP 10 BEACHES

1)   Railay Beach – Krabi (West Beach)

Part of the mainland of Krabi, Railay is cut off by mountain landscapes and only accessible by boat. There are no cars and it has the feel of a small island. The West beach and surrounding scenery is easily one of the most dramatic and beautiful in Thailand. The beach itself has soft golden sands, emerald green waters, and is lined with palm trees and limestone cliffs which create a bay. Just a little bit further inland at walking street and you will find plenty of restaurants, bars, and shops set up in wooden structures. Rock climbing is very popular here, but if you're not that adventurous there is still much to do and see on the beach and surrounding areas.

Photo Credit Jakub Barzycki/shutterstock.com

It is only around a 10 minute walk from the west beach to the east beach. The east beach is in complete contrast to the west, with local fishing boats and mangrove landscapes. The Phra Nang Cave Beach is also in walking distance from the west beach. Due to Railay being such a beautiful destination it is also very popular, so expect crowds to follow. One way to get around this is to stay overnight as many of the people here are day trippers which return in the late afternoon.

TOP TIP: Stay at least one night for the best experience.

2)   Klong Jark Beach - Koh Lanta

If you're looking to escape the crowds and enjoy some peace and quiet, Klong Jark is worth the visit. Due to its remote location, this small beach in the south of Koh Lanta remains largely undeveloped or visited. Don't expect it to be completely deserted though, as it does have a few small resorts and beach bars. With white sand, clear blue waters, and peaceful atmosphere, it's easily one of Koh Lanta's most naturally stunning beaches.

Photo Credit Denis Costillie /shutterstock.com

The water is shallow inshore and protected by the bay, so snorkelling and kayaking are great options. As well as enjoying the beach, a small trek from here will take you to a waterfall. It's worth noting that if you cant get to this beach, Koh lanta is full of many other stunning and hardly touched beaches. The community of Koh lanta has largely manged to escape the highend commercial side of tourism.

TOP TIP: Do not to get this beach confused with the one on Koh Yao Noi, which is also called Klong Jark.

3)   Lonely Beach – Koh Chang

This beach is one of the best places to stay if you want to meet other travellers and stay on the actual beach in reasonably affordable accommodation. It is well known for being the best beach for backpackers, but now you can find anything from 3-star resorts to beach bungalows, so it is slowly drawing different crowds.

Photo Credit Nataliia Sokolovska /shutterstock.com

As well as accommodation, there are good options for restaurants and bars. The nearby village offers even more choice and extra activities. Despite the name, it has a very lively and friendly atmosphere which carries on into the night. Great beach parties are to be had here, with many beach side bars and resturants provding entertainment. The beach itself is relatively small, spanning only a few hundred metres.

TOP TIP: If you are looking to book a hotel on Koh Chang and want to stay close by or on Lonley beach, Oasis Koh Chang or Nest sense resort are great options.

4)   Lamai Beach - Koh Samui

This beach is a perfect mix of popularity and having plenty of things to do without being over crowded due to its size. The beach is lined with resorts, restaurants, bars, and vendors. You can get massages and manicures with ease and water sports are available as well as diving and tours.

Photo Credit SMIRNOVA IRINA/shutterstock.com

The water is clear and has netted areas for the safety of tourists and locals. The beach has soft sands and is lined with palm trees. If you're looking for somewhere to be entertained but want to avoid massive crowds, this is the beach for you. It has a more laid-back atmosphere but with plenty of options for things to do. It is also a family-friendly beach. Although there will be many people here, its long stretch of golden sands give plenty of space.

TOP TIP: If renting a Jet ski check out the Top Ten tips chapter on how to do this in the best possible way.

5)   Soneva Kiri resort - Koh Kood

Making the top 10 due to it being one of the most well-kept and cleanest beaches in Thailand (possibly the world), is the beach at Soneva Kiri resort. Like many of the other beaches mentioned, it has everything you could want, from soft sand to crystal clear waters. Because it is one of the best resorts in Thailand, it is very well maintained. It also has some amazing views which reach out across the sea to the neighbouring island, Koh Mai Sai. Unfortunately, due to it being a resort beach you would need to stay at the Soneva Kiri to enjoy it. The Soneva Kiri is also featured in the top 10 alternative activities, so why not pair the two together? A visit here is best suited to a more mature age group or couples looking for that romantic getaway.

Photo Credit Travel_Leap / Soneva Brand centre

TOP TIP: Check out the Top Ten Alternative chapter to see how you can make this already luxurious experience even more incredible.

6)   Patong Beach – Phuket

Some will be wondering how the hell Patong made the top ten. Well, the top 10 is as much about variety as it is picking out the very best of places, and Patong beach has exactly that variety. It is action-packed with water sports and activities and it is one of the easiest beaches to find and access. The amount of other amenities available will keep all age ranges and interests entertained. There is parking close by, public toilets, and life guards are normally on patrol.

Photo Credit aphotostory /shutterstock.com

The beach, although often busy, still has soft golden sands lined with palm trees and clear blue waters. If you're looking for a beach to keep you excited and entertained, Patong beach is a great choice. If the crowds do get to be too much, it is also very easy to book excursions and trips from here.

7) Koh Mak

Koh Mak is actually an island, but due to the small size and ease of getting around, I've decided not to single out a particular beach. The charm of Koh Mak comes from it being mostly undeveloped and a lesser known destination for tourists. If you're looking for a quiet getaway beach that helps you feel disconnected from the outside world, Koh Mak will provide this for you.

Photo Credit DeltaOFF/shutterstock.com

There are a few resort restaurants and shops on the island, but make sure you bring cash with you. To get around this small island you can use the shuttle buses, taxis, or rent a push bike and explore at your own pace. Head northwest for the most undeveloped areas. If you're looking for a relaxing beach with a little bit of life and some facilities then head to Ao Kao.

TOP TIP: Take cash to this island.

8)   Sai Nuan – Koh Tao

The island of Koh Tao is famous for its excellent diving and snorkelling spots and Sai Nuan beach is no exception. With no roads leading directly to it, it is only accessible via hiking trails or boat, and as a result has kept its natural beauty and is not normally crowded. Its back drop of large rocks and jungle scenery gives this beach an idyllic tropical island feel.

Photo Credit mistudiodesign /shutterstock.com

There are a few small beach huts, hammocks, and swings to help complete that picture-perfect scene. Be sure to take your snorkels as the corals are only a few metres from shore. You will witness an array of underwater life, including many species of fish, sea turtles, and even black tip reef sharks as they are common here. It's also worth mentioning this is actually two beaches which are separated by a rocky out crop, so be sure to explore a little further than the first beach you arrive at.

TOP TIP: Bring some snoorkeling equipment to this beach.

9)   Mae Haad – Koh Phangan

With shallow waters and plenty of small reefs, this an ideal spot for snorkelling and spotting underwater life. This beach has long sand banks, clear waters with different shades of blue, and a surrounding landscape that screams tropical island paradise! But there is one thing that makes this beach unique; at low tide you can walk along a slim sand bank which leads you to a small island called Ko Ma.

Photo Credit Anaa Ewa Bieniek /shutterstock.com

The island is protected and open to the public to explore and add a bit of adventure to their visit. Along the main beach you can find a few bars and restaurants to keep you refreshed throughout the day. Although Mae Haad attracts many visitors, it has a pretty laid-back vibe and is not so overly crowded that you have to fight for a spot in the sun.

10)   Morakot cave (emerald cave) - Ko Muk

This beach is only accessible by swimming 18 metres though a cave, and if the tide is low enough, by kayaks and small boats. Once you are through you will be rewarded by being in one of the most surreal and unique beaches in Thailand.

Photo Credit Arnon Polin/shutterstock.com

The small sandy beach and clear shallow waters are completely encompassed by towering limestone cliffs and tropical plants hanging from the edges. A large opening at the top of the cliffs allows enough light for you to enjoy your surroundings. It does get quite crowded here, partly because it's quite a popular destination and partly because it's a small beach.

TOP TIP: To beat the crowds, try hiring a private long tail boat early in the morning.

CHAPTER 3 TOP 10 NATIONAL PARKS

1)   Khao Sok

Although the area of Khao Sok is known as one of the wettest parts of Thailand, the National park here is also one of the most popular for tourists, and for good reason too. It is one of the most easily accessible national parks, with regular transport and transfers from Krabi, Phuket and Surat Thani. Here you can expect to discover waterfalls, find thick luscious rain forests homing many exotic plant species, and the good chance of seeing serval types of monkeys and birds. If you are really lucky, you may even witness wild cats and wild elephants in their natural habitat.

Photo Credit martinho smart/shutterstock.com

One of the most stunning features of the park is the glorious Cheow Larn lake. Surrounded by green jungle and dramatic limestone mountains, it really is a sight to be seen. The sunsets here are said to be some of the most beautiful in Thailand, and even the world. You can actually stay overnight on the lake here. There are a mix of standard floating bungalows to the more up-market, floating, glamping-style camps. Everything is made accessible and easy to arrange, from guided jungle treks to renting a kayak in which to explore the lake.

Opening Times: 7am -7pm Although some overnight trekking and lake tours are available, as well as accomodations.
Entrance Fee: Yes

2)   Kaeng Krachan National Park

Thailand's largest National park which borders with Burma really has it all! From trekking and hiking through the rain forests to exploring caves and natural pools to take a dip in, you will not be disappointed here. There are amazing waterfalls, rock climbing opportunities and many rivers and lakes from which you can take boat rides down. Accommodation and campsites are available which allow you to stay within the national park. As well as being well known for its variety of activities, it is also well known for the diverse wildlife, in particular butterflies and birds.

Photo Credit Blue Sky Studio /shutterstock.com

Around 400 species of birds have been recorded here, including rare breeds such as the whooly-necked stork, giant pitta, and great argus. Although harder to come across, the park is also home to endangered animals such as tigers, the Asiatic leopard, wild elephants, and wild dogs. All in all, this is a true dream come true for nature lovers and adventure travellers alike! It's important to note that you are not allowed to trek these vast lands by yourself and must hire an experienced local guide.

TOP TIP: Hire a guide to take you deep into this vast national park.

Opening Times: 6am – 6pm Although accomodation and camp sites are 24hrs you will be restricted to these areas. **Entrance Fee:** Yes

3)   Erawan National Park

Located in the province of Kanchanaburi, Erawan National Park is relatively easy to access from Bangkok, and is most famous for its seven-tier waterfall and emerald green waters. Each tier of the waterfall provides a small natural pool to swim in and slightly different features. Keep an eye out for the small fish that gently nibble your feet. The bottom pools get quite busy, but if you're a little bit active, take the opportunity to climb higher up to the lesser visited pools. The top tier of the falls is meant to represent the 3 headed Hindu elephant god, Erawan, hence the name "Erawan Falls".

Photo Credit SUWIT NGAOKAEW/shutterstock.com

One of the great things about this national park is that you don't have to be overly active to travel so far into the park to get to the falls and enjoy nature. The first pool created by the falls is on the same level as the picnic area. You can either bring food with you or buy from one of the small pop up stalls, but be aware that sometimes there are cheeky monkeys about that will try and take your food and drink. Of course, the park is not just about the falls; you can stay here in bungalows or at the campsite near the visitor centre. Options to rent and ride bikes are also available.

Opening Times: 8am - 4.30pm
Entrance Fee: Yes

4)   Mu Ko Ang Thong National Park

Unlike the inland and rainforest type national parks, Mu Ko Ang Thong is more about sun, sand and sea. Located in the gulf of Thailand and west of Koh Samui, this is a marine national park comprising of 42 islands. A visit here is best taken by a guided tour boat or even a personally rented boat. The variety of landscapes here are attractive and interesting in themselves. Some islands will deliver scenes of idyllic white sand beaches whilst others have vast mountain landscapes.

Photo Credit Pavinee Chareonpanich /shutterstock.com

As it's a marine park, the variety of mammals and birds here are quite limited compared to many of the above options. However, this is compensated by the many great snorkelling spots and a blue lagoon which will have you in awe. A visit here is perfect for someone who wants to take in a little bit of nature and marine life whilst kicking back and relaxing at the same time. It's worth mentioning that there is an awesome view point here, with stunning views of the above, as far as the eye can see.

TOP TIP: Check out the view point for the best views of this national park.

Opening Times: 8am – 5pm
Entrance Fee: Yes, some areas of land

5)   Hat Chao Mai National Park

Located in the southwest corner of Thailand and part of the Trang province lies the Hat Chao Mai National park. This is another marine national park. Due to its location, you will often find much fewer tourists here with food and activities at a much cheaper rate. Compared to many of the other national parks, Hat Chao Mai inland areas and landscapes are nothing that spectacular! If you are a nature lover or wildlife enthusiast, a visit here will provide the chance of seeing the very rare and endangered sea mammal, the Dugong.

Photo Credit Tommy Johansson/shutterstock.com

A Dugong is closely related to the manatee but lives in sea water opposed to fresh water. These sea mammals are calm, peaceful and fun to watch. The area was established in 1981 and is protected. As a result, some impressive coral reef systems can be found here. It is a great location for spotting many marine species, including seahorses and the mentioned Dugong.

Opening Times: 9am – 4pm
Entrance Fee: Yes

6)   Si Phang Nga National Park

Often referred to as the little Amazon, Si Phang Nga is one of Thailand's oldest rainforests and actually older than the Amazon itself. Due to its age, it has an interesting array of plants and flora. The park also provides the opportunity to spot many bird species which are harder to find in many parts of Southern Thailand. A great thing to do here is hire inflatable boats and paddle down the river which leads you to a beautiful waterfall. The pools of water at the bottom of the waterfall are full of freshwater fish. Lots of the fish are of a good size and present great photo opportunities.

Photo Credit Don Mammoser/shutterstock.com

Many mammal species can also be found here, which include barking deer, Malay tapir, macaque, langur, gibbon, and even the lesser mouse-deer! The lesser mouse-deer can be as small as 45cm at mature age. If you were to ever see a photo of one and not really know about them you may think it's photoshopped or fake.

Like many of the national parks in Thailand, there is accommodation and camping areas if you decide a day trip is not enough, or you just like the idea of a peaceful atmosphere and nature's sounds throughout the night.

Opening Times: 8am – 4pm
Entrance Fee: Yes

7)   Doi Inthanon National Park

Doi Inthanon, which is also known as "the roof top of Thailand," is very popular for its waterfalls, viewpoints, and mountain landscapes. It is in fact actually part of the Himalayan mountain range. The highest peak in Thailand is located here at a height of 2565 metres. One of the most impressive waterfalls, named Mae Yai, pours over a 100-metre drop. Due to its location and height above sea level, this national park is much cooler in temperature than any of the others, which can be a nice break from the heat. Be prepared; in cool season, the mountains and other areas can easily hit negative temperatures, so it is best avoided at this time of year.

As well as providing a home for wildlife, Doi Inthanon is also home to Northern Hill tribes. Although there is increasing tourism and modern Thailand is encroaching, many efforts are being put in place to encourage the hill tribes to live a traditional life and keep ancient cultural ways alive. Another difference with this national park is that there are two Chedis (monuments) which sit upon the hills and were constructed to celebrate the Kings and Queens 60th birthdays. The detailed architecture and impressive back drops are pefecting for taking photos that scream Thailand.

TOP TIP: Visit early to view a either a stunning sunset or a magical sea of clouds.
Opening Times: 6am – 6pm.
Entrance Fee: Yes

8)   Mu ko Surin National Park

This national park is made up of a collection of protected islands in the Andaman sea, which are located around 37 miles from the mainland and west coast of Thailand. Whilst it hosts some beautiful white sand beaches and thick green jungles, the main highlight of a visit here is snorkelling and scuba diving. It is one of the few locations in Thailand where you have a good chance of seeing and swimming with species such as manta rays, barracudas, and whale sharks.

Photo Credit Jamesboy Nuchaikong /shutterstock.com

If you do take a trip here for the snorkelling and diving, be sure to check out Richelieu Rock, which is a horseshoe-shaped reef and famous spot for diving. It is where you will have the better chance of seeing the above named species. Also, if you want to see sea turtles, check out turtle ledge / turtle ridge for your best chances. Another interesting activity is visiting the close by Moken village. The Moken people are an ancient nomadic sea tribe. They spend a vast majority of their lives either on or in the sea; many are even born on boats. The Moken are hunters and gatherers of the sea with eye sight which work twice as well under water than the rest of the human species. It's also important to know these are not Thai Citizens, but a very ancient people that claim no nationality, which makes them even more interesting.

Opening Times: 24hrs (sea areas) Land opening times differ
Entrance Fee: Yes to some land areas

9)   Kui Buri National Park

Located in the Prachuap Khiri Khan Province, the Kui Buri national park made my top ten for one main reason, and that is because this is the best national park In Thailand for seeing wild elephants. If it's your dream to see Asian elephants in all their natural glory and not chained up as part of a tourist attraction, Kui Buri is your best bet. Whilst it can never be guaranteed, it is definitely worth giving it a go. Even better, this national park can only be explored by African-style safaris. This is perfect for those less able to hike in the humidity or over difficult terrain.

Photo Credit Tanongsak Sangthong /shutterstock.com

All in all you still get to enjoy the wildlife and landscapes but in a more stress free, safe, and accessible way. You will also get the opportunity to get out of the vehicles and stretch your legs at designated viewing points. The landscapes you will drive through are mainly large areas of grass lands with mountain backdrops, and you may also pass some small rivers and lakes. The visitor centre and facilities are very basic, as is the campsite area, but as mentioned at the start, a visit here is all about seeing those beautiful gentle giants.

TOP TIP: Visit Late afternoon or early morning when wildlife is more active.

Opening Times: 07.00 – 18.00 Although accomodations and camp site are 24hrs you will be restricted to these areas. **Entrance Fee**: Yes

10)   Khao Yai National Park

Khao Yai is similar to the above Kui Buri in the sense that you have a very good chance of seeing wild elephants here. In fact, I would rank it around 2nd place for the best opportunity. The park also offers many hiking trails to be enjoyed, magnificent waterfalls to be viewed, and a mixture of landscapes from grasslands to evergreen jungles and mountain areas. The park has a good level of facilities including basic accommodation and restaurants.

Photo Credit dsy88 /shutterstock.com

Like Kui Buri, it also offers driving safari options with an added bonus of a night safari available. The park also homes many other animals such as gibbons, macaque, porcupines, civet, and barking & sambar deer. Reptiles are also quite common here as you can find Ahaetulla prasina, crested lizards, Chinese water dragons, water monitors, Reticulated pythons and Chinese rat snakes. As for birds, the park is home to around 300 species, which includes one of Thailand's largest hornbill populations. If you're looking for a mix between having a good chance of seeing a wild elephant but with variety of other animals, a range of different landscapes, and a little more freedom, Khao Yai is perfect.

Opening times: 07.00 -17.00 Although some over night trekking / safari Tours are available, as well as accomodations.
Entrance Fee: Yes

CHAPTER 4 TOP 10 MARKETS

1)   Chatuchak Weekend Market – Bangkok

Classified as one of the largest weekend markets in the world, Chatuchak has actually become a landmark in itself for visitors in Bangkok. There are over 8000 stalls, which are sectioned off into 27 main areas covering 35 acres and attracting 200,000 visitors daily. There really is something for everyone here, from handcrafted items and clothes, to electronics, antiques, toys, plants, art, and collectibles. This never-ending list even includes animals such as snakes and kittens.

Photo Credit atapartment/shutterstock.com

You will be spoiled with choices with the different merchandise, and most likely leave with things that you never thought about, let alone were looking to buy. This is a great place to brush up on your bargaining skills. If you can't get the price you want at a particular stall, then it's highly likely you will find other stores selling the exact same thing you just walked away from; so bargain away! Like with most Thai markets, there are plenty of places to stop and relax. This market also offers a wide range of massage parlours and restaurants.

Opening times: Saturday and Sunday 9am-6pm (Whole Market open)
Friday 6pm-12pm (Wholesale only)
Wednesday and Thursday 7am-6pm (Plant section only)

2)   Phuket Walking Street night market

Established in 2013 and stretching over 350m, this market is relatively small compared with the above Chatuchak. Having said this, it does not lack in character and charm. It is set alongside Sino Portuguese-style houses, which are lit up with different coloured lights. It almost makes you feel as though you are caught up in a cross between Mediterranean Europe and Asia.

Photo Credit BREEZY STOCK/shutterstock.com

The market's main sales come from people looking for street food and souvenirs, though you can often find street performances such as dancing and live music, which adds to great atmosphere. The houses on either side of the street are home to many shops, bars, and restaurants, including Phuket's oldest pharmacy. Many of the stall holders are young entrepreneurs who are producing creative and fun handcrafted products. Given the smaller size, early start time of this night market and a more laid-back pace, it is quite a family-friendly place to go to.

TOP TIP: Make sure you bring cash to all markets, it is very rare street vendors are able to except card payments.

Opening Hours: Every Sunday from 16:00 – 22:00
Location: Thalang Road in Phuket Old Town

3)   Rod Fai -Train Night Market Ratchada

Located in a vintage and hip location, this market is very popular with younger generations and Thai locals. This is great, as prices here are lower compared to many other Bangkok markets (although I still advise a bit of bargaining). It may not be as touristy here, but there are still many interesting things to see and buy. Running between 3 main sois (streets), you can find anything from second-hand and vintage items to new clothes, shoes, and fashion accessories.

Photo Credit Hit1912/shutterstock.com

One of the best parts of a visit here is the atmosphere. The streets are lined with numerous bars and places to eat with live music. You can also find vintage VW vans that play a good mix of Thai and western pop music. It has a very laid back and friendly feel to it. Perfect for younger solo travellers looking to make friends whilst exploring and doing a bit of shopping at the same time.

Opening Hours: 17:00-24:00 (Thursday-Sunday)
Location: Ratcadaphisek Road (close to Esplanade Shopping Mall)
MRT: National Cultural Centre

4)   Damnoen Saduak Floating Market - Ratchaburi Province

This is one of Thailand's largest and most popular floating markets. It dates back over 100 years and is located approximately 1.5 hours from Bangkok. Here you will find most things that you would come across in the average Thai street market, but most people visit here for the experience of shopping whilst on a boat. The food here is tasty, with plenty of freshly made dishes and fresh produce for you to indulge in.

Photo c sa bum /shutterstock.com

There are often great photo opportunities along the way, especially as you pass the lines of boats loaded with colourful produce. Due to being so popular, Damnoen Saduak floating market has become more of a tourist attraction rather than an authentic Thai experience. It is busy and fast paced, with a loud and buzzing atmosphere. On a visit to this market, many tour operators will include a visit to an orchard farm and coconut plantation along the way, adding variation to your day out. This makes for a plus point!

Opening Hours: 06.30 – 11.00 Daily
Location: Tambon Damnoen Saduak, Amphoe Damnoen Saduak, Ratchaburi Province.

5)   Maeklong Railway Market (Talad Rom Hub)

This traditional, yet unconventional Thai market sells everything from fresh fruit and vegetables to fish and meats, although it is best known for its seafood. However, what makes it unique is its location. It is located right on a live railway track, on which a handful of trains pass through each day. All the produce sold here is on either side of the track. Vendors can be seen quickly covering their produce and lowering their make shift roofs as the train passes through. It really is quite a sight and it is impressive how nothing gets damaged as the train passes through the market. Although this place is a little more off the beaten path, it offers an insight into daily life in Thailand.

Photo Credit puwanai /shutterstock.com

TOP TIP: If you want to see the actual train passing through, check the most up to date timetable, and allow 30minutes either side of this time.

Opening Times: 04.00 – 17.00
Location: Si Champa Alley, Samut Songkhram 75000, Thailand.

6)   Night Bazaar / Anusarn Market- Chiang Mai

This market is open every night, hence why it has been included in the top 10. This makes it convenient for travellers who don't want to dedicate a specific night to experience a night market. What makes it different than other markets are the locally handcrafted products and authentic northern cuisine on sale. Things here can be relatively cheap, giving you even more reason to visit it. Like any other market, there are plenty of food stalls to experince and live music to enjoy, all of which really adds to the atomosphere. If you can't find what you are looking for, the surrounding areas of the market are also great for adding even more options for eating, drinking and shopping.

Photo Credit joyfull/shutterstock.com

TOP TIP: Make sure you try the food offered at the Ansusarn market section.

Opening times: Everyday 5pm – 12am
Location: 104/1 intersection of Tha Pae and Chang Klan Road | Chang Klang, Chiang Mai 50100, Thailand

7) Khlong Lat Mayom Floating / River Market

In contrast to the touristy Damnoen Saduak Floating Market, the Khlong Lat Mayom Floating Market has a much more authentic feel to it. If you visit it at the right time you may very well be one of a few tourists there. It is a bit smaller compared to other floating markets in Thailand and is made up of river side stalls. You can find merchants selling produce and cooking food from their boats. Its reputation prides itself on offering a large selection of fresh and organic produce. In addition to the food, you can also find cheap authentic clothing, toys, flowers, and traditional furniture..

Photo Credit Denis Costille/shutterstock.com

You will also have the opportunity for boat tours. A boat tour here will offer an insight into rural areas whilst exploring in and around the khlongs (canal neighbourhood). There is also a ranch close by that you could visit with children. If you're looking for a more authentic market and want a insider's view of local life then Khlong Lat Mayom is a brilliant option

Opening Times: Saturdays, Sundays and public holidays from 9:30 am to 4:30 pm.
Location: Soi Bang Ramat | Bang Ramat, Taling Chan, Bangkok 10170, Thailand

8)   Yaowarat - Bangkok

This might not be what you would be expecting to find in the top 10 Market chapter. However, how could the best food market in Bangkok not be included. A visit here is a must for any food lover! It is made up of a mixture of street food carts, stalls and restaurants which pour out into the streets. It is based in China town, so a lot of the food has a chinese influence, although many authentic Thai dishes are still on offer. If you are a seafood lover then this is also the place to visit. It offers a vast selection of dishes that will not disappoint. The best advice is to pace yourself and try many different dishes along the way.

Photo Credit MR. SUTTICHAI CHALOKUL /shutterstock.com

An interesting fact about Yaowarat is that it is home to many vendors which are on the Michelin star street food guide. Award winning Auntie Jai Fais, is only a 10 mintues taxi ride from here. This popular vendor has a lot to offer with prices being slightly more expensive. Apart from Auntie Jai Fais, other market stalls/street food vendors are fairly reasonably priced. Be prepared to have your senses overloaded and taste buds tingling!

Opening Times: These vary from early in the am to late at night, the best time to go is early evening through to around 10pm.
Location: Yaowarat Road Bangkok

9)   Krabi Town night Maket

With handmade crafts, souvenirs, art, toys, clothes, fashion items, street food, and local produce all available, Krabi town night market is very similar to other markets. So, what makes it different? Well, the main thing that stands out here is the open-air seating area. It comprises of many seats and a good-sized performance stage. With different performances on each night, you can enjoy a welcomed break from all the shopping and eating. Performances can include anything from cultural shows to local Thai bands, which really boosts the atmosphere of this market. This also provides an opportunity for local schools and children to perform. The area of Krabi in general is less touristic compared to other southern destinations like Phuket, and is generally cheaper, although that often depends on your bartering skills!

Photo Credit fivepointsix/shutterstock.com

TOP TIP: For all markets make sure you barter, but barter with a smile!

Opening Hours: Fri, Sat & Sun from 17:00-22:00
Location: Soi Maharaj 8 (behind Vogue Department Store)

10)   MBK Center – Bangkok

Many outdoor markets have been mentioned in the top 10 so in case of rain or you've simply had enough of the heat, the MBK center needs to be included. More of a hybrid between a shopping mall and a market, MBK is spread over 8 floors and has around 2000 shops/stalls, offering clothing, food, souvenirs, electronics, furniture, and much more. Prices here can be a little more than in street markets but are cheaper than in actual shopping malls. The complex also includes a designated food court and entertainment section. So, if you fancy catching a movie in the cinema, playing some computer games, or singing some karaoke in between shopping, you can. You can also find beauty and hair salons here. Compared to some other markets, it is easy to navigate and find your way around here as it has many clear signs and an organized layout.

Photo Credit Panya7 /shutterstock.com

Opening Hours: 10:00 - 22:00
Location: Pathumwan Intersection, diagonally opposite Siam Discovery Centre.

CHAPTER 5 TOP 10 FESTIVALS

1) SONGKRAN – THE WATER FESTIVAL

The Songkran festival is one of Thailand's most widely celebrated festivals. It is quite literally a 3-day nationwide water fight. This festival has to be one of the most fun and craziest festivals you will ever experience. During Songkran, you will never be far from some kind of exciting celebration. This festival is meant for all to enjoy and get involved in, Thais and westerners alike. It is not all water fights either. There will be merit-making ceremonies, concerts, and parades to be found. Some very impressive firework displays often take place later in the evening. However, be warned that no one is safe. You will be confronted with water pistols, water bombs, buckets of water, hoses, and anything that can be filled with water. What is a better way to cool down in one of Thailand's hottest months? As wild as it sounds, the Songkran festival actually originates from Buddhist tradition. It marks Buddhist new year and splashing water is a sign of purification. With this in mind, please remember that this is classed as a bank holiday.

Photo Credit artapartment /shutterstock.com

Dates: 13th, 14th and 15th of April Every Year

Specific locations: Bangkok Khosan Road and Silom Road, Chaing Mai Tha Pae Gate old city, Phuket Soi Bangla, Pattaya Beach Street, Koh Samui Chaweng Beach, Krabi Ao Nang Beach Road

2) Yi PENG – THE LANTERN FESTIVAL

The Lantern Festival really is one of the most mesmerizing, peaceful, and magical festivals you will ever experience. If you are looking for the perfect photo opportunity and that feel good feeling, this is the festival for you. The main highlight of this festival is, of course, the mass release of thousands of lanterns at once, gently floating away and lighting up the night sky with a warm glow. However, there will be many fireworks, parades, traditional music, and religious ceremonies to enjoy.

Photo Credit nuwatphoto /shutterstock.com

Although many provinces in Thailand will celebrate Yi Peng, Chaing Mai is the go to destination to experience it in its entirety. Yi Peng is celebrated in line with Loy Krathong and spans over 3 days; the exact date is always subject to change as it is to fall on the full moon of the 12th month of the Thai Lunar calendar (usually November). As with many of the festivals celebrated in Thailand, it is important to remember this is not meant as a tourist attraction but is a religious and cultural celebration.

Location: Chaing Mai
Dates: November on the full moon of the 12th month of the Thai lunar calendar

3) Loy Krathong

Thailand's 2nd most famous and widely celebrated festivals. The main activity at the Loy Krathong festival is the release of small, stunning lotus shaped rafts into a body of water. Each raft will also have a lit candle placed upon it, along with incense. These are called a "krathong," and are commonly released into rivers, lakes, and ponds by hundreds, if not thousands, of participants at a time. The sheer number of these tiny krathongs set against the shimmering back drop of the night's water, is a magical sight to be seen. This will often be accompanied by fireworks, music, and sometimes dance performances. Over the years, krathongs have been criticised for being harmful to the environment. As a result, bio-degradable options are available.

Photo Credit Jakkraphat /shutterstock.com

There are many different stories for the meanings behind Loy Krathong. One of the most common meanings being it is a way of showing respect and making merit to the water goddess. Many Thais also see it as a way to rid themselves of bad fortune, lust, and selfishness, by floating away these troubles on the krathong.

Location: Nation wide
Dates: November on the full moon of the 12th month of the Thai lunar calendar

4) BOON BANG FAI – THE ROCKET FESTIVAL

If you like fireworks (rockets), big bangs, and a loud excitable environment, this festival is for you. The Rocket Festival is a little more off the beaten path than the likes of Sonkran or Yi Peng. It is held by the farming communities of Northeastern Thailand (Issan), with the largest of events being celebrated in the Yasothon Province. The festival starts with the first day consisting of parades which show off the rockets. During this period there will be plenty of traditional Thai folk music, dancing, and local rice wine to be enjoyed adding to the excitement of the festival..

Photo Credit Worachat Sodsri/shutterstock.com

The large rockets that are all homemade in different styles are fired into the air with extreme force, spinning rapidly and reaching far heights creating an exciting display. The builders of the highest reaching rocket will be declared the winner of this event. In the unfortunate event that a rocket misfires and does not launch you can witness the builder of the said rockets being playfully thrown in the mud. Boon Ban Fai is an ancient festival which takes place to inspire the Gods to bless the farmers with abundant rains for prized rice crops

Location: Yasothon Province / North Eastern Thailand
Dates: Around Middle of May, exact dates are not confirmed until up to a few weeks before, as they are determined by the Thai lunar calander

5) LOPBURI MONKEY FESTIVAL

150km North of Bangkok is the city of Lopburi. It is best known for its large monkey population, with troops of them often getting up to no good. The city is full of ancient ruins as it thought to be over 3000 years old. Every year on the last Sunday of November, a feast is laid out for the monkeys. Rows upon rows of tables are laid out with colourful displays of fruits and food. This attracts around 3000 monkeys into a complete feeding frenzy. Tourists and locals alike get the chance to get up close and personal with these cheeky little guys with plenty of amazing photo opportunities arising.

Photo Credit topten22photo/shutterstock.com

The monkeys are not shy by any means and will try and take anything they can get their hands on, including your wallet, sunglasses, or ice cream. Please be aware and secure anything valuable. When interacting with the monkeys, it is important to remember that they are wild animals. Many Thais believe that the monkeys are a direct descendant of Hanuman the Hindu God, and therefore They hold religious significance. This festival and the city of Lopburi is best suited to animal lovers and fans of history.

Location: Lopburi
Date: Last Sunday of each November

6) PHI TA KHON – GHOST FESTIVAL

This 3-day festival is set in the small town of Dan Sai (Loei Province), and is a little bit off the beaten path, so try and plan ahead if you want to attend. The main highlight of the ghost festival is the parade that takes place in town. Hundreds of locals gather, wearing handmade masks that resemble ghosts. The masks are elaborate and brightly painted with wonderful colours. Over the three-day period there is a mixture of events including games, pageants, concerts, and Buddhist ceremonies.

Photo Credit Suryia99 /shutterstock.com

The atmosphere can best be described as fun, energetic and uplifting. It is believed that this festival is a mix of Buddhist and animist beliefs. The main aim is to throw a party so fun that both the living and dead, human or animal, will want to come. The town of Dan Sai is located in the northeast part of Thailand and is surrounded by a few national parks. It is perfect for the adventurous type who wants to experience a unique festival whilst taking in some beautiful scenery and nature along the way. It's worth noting that dressing up as a ghost is optional, but very welcomed if you do decide to.

Location: Dan Sai, Loei Province
Date: The weekend of the 6th full moon of the lunar calendar (starting on Friday)

7) WING KWAI – BUFFALO RACING FESTIVAL

The tradition of the buffalo racing festival has been taking place in Chonburi for well over one hundred years. More recently, it has begun to attract even more crowds, adding to the excitement and atmosphere. The buffalos are raced down a 100m track, accompanied by their jockey riding bare back and pushing these large beasts along. This is a skill to be witnessed with your own eyes. As well as the main event of the buffalo race, the day consists of beauty contests, Muay Thai (Thai boxing) demonstrations, fair rides for children, and fete games for all, some of which are quite funny to watch. This is a fun family-orientated festival which is fairly easy to get to compared to some of the other top 10 selections. However, you will still feel slightly off the beaten path.

Photo Credit Mr.Suchat/shutterstock.com

TOP TIP: This festival runs over several day's, but the main race day is by far the most fun.

Location: Chonburi opposite the city hall.
Date: Usually held in October, however it is held in line with the Buddhist lent and lunar calendar therefore dates will vary from year to year.

8) KIN JAY - THE VEGETARIAN FESTIVAL

The Kin Jay festival usually runs for the last 9 days of October in Phuket with the main ceremonies taking place at the Jui Tu Shrine. During this period, many parts of Phuket will be decorated with bright yellow and red flags and banners, symbolising the dedication and participation of this festival. There is a plentiful supply of fresh vegetarian food, with a large variety of options from dim sum to noodles, curries to dumplings, leaf wrapped parcels to spicy stir fries. There really is something for everyone. Despite the name, this festival is full of gruesome and terrifying displays. These include self impalement to the face and parts of the body with sharp objects. Experienced performers use anything from swords to large pins. These acts also include walking over red-hot coals.

Photo Credit MR.Suksan Samranrit/shutterstock.com

The reason for these acts is believed to have originated from Chinese beliefs. The self harm is seen as a kind of sacrifice, which will in turn bring protection from the Gods and scare away evil spirts. As exciting and interesting as this all may sound, it is definitely not designed for the faint of heart. Those who take part are expected to wear white and give up all meat, fish, sex, and alcohol for the duration of the 9 days.

Location: Phuket town / Jui Tu Shrine
Date: Usually the last 9 days of October

9) CHINESE NEW YEAR (Bangkok)

Chinese New Year is widely celebrated in Bangkok. The main action is located around Yaowarat Road, which is Bangkok's China town. During this period, the already lively Yaowarat road explodes with life and celebrations. Crowds of worshippers flock to this destination, filling the entire length of the road and even the smaller connecting sois (streets) and alleys. The scene is set with buildings decorated with red flags and banners. It becomes a fun and vibrant location, with dragon dancers putting on performances and parades proceeding down the road. Random fire crackers are set off by the crowds, whilst loud processions of drums can be heard warning of bad luck and the evil spirits.

Photo Credit Cowardlion /shutterstock.com

To think this festival couldn't offer any more, Yaowarat street is already famous for its street food, and the celebrations of Chinese New Year are no exception. Extra efforts are put into provding some of Bangkok's very best street food. You will also find sumptuous Chinese banquets that wouldn't be found every day. All your senses are forced to come alive.

Location: Bangkok Yaowarat Road.

Dates: Based on the Chinese Luna calendar and confirmed year to year (usually falls between January to February)

10) THE CANDLE FESTIVAL

This festival really incorporates artistic creativity and culture into its celebrations. The name hints that candles are involved. These, however, are not just any old candles, these are giant candle sculptures based on Thai mythology. They are created by highly skilled artisan teams, and take weeks to complete. The intricate wax works are then paraded through the streets with the best design winning prizes. Like with many Thai festivals, the candle festival holds religious importance, and is held in line with the Buddhist events Asahna Bucha and Khao Phansa. Although this is a Buddhist holiday, you will still experience a very lively and upbeat atmosphere with plenty of dancing and traditional folk music to keep you entertained. In between, you will have the chance to view the spectacular wax sculptures. The tradition dates back to a time when electricity was not yet invented and candles were a good method of donating to the temples.

Photo Credit Worakit Sirijinda /shutterstock.com

Location: Thung Si Mueang Park in central Ubon Ratchathani. Also on the day of Khao Phansa, a huge street parade commences from outside (temple) Wat Sri Ubon Rattanaram and proceeds north along Upparat Road.

Date: Based on the Thai Lunar calendar and in line with Asahna Bucha and Khao Phansa day, so will vary from year to year but will usually fall in July.

CHAPTER 6 TOP 10 PARTY SPOTS

1) Khao San Road – Bangkok

Spread out over a 1-kilometre strip, Khao San Road is best known as the backpacker central of the world. Having said that, you don't need to be one to enjoy a good evening/night out here. With so much to offer from live music, karaoke bars, organised bar crawls, shisha bars, pubs and clubs, it attracts a wide variety of people and age ranges including Thai locals. It is the perfect place to meet other people if you are a solo traveller or even if you are travelling in a group. The variety of places to eat and drink is great and prices are reasonable.

Photo Credit Hafiz Johari /shutterstock.com

The atmosphere can be best described as carefree, full of life, and unique to this part of Bangkok. As well as places to party, Khao San has many hostels, tour operators, shops, street food carts, market stalls and restaurants. It's worth the visit even if for just one night, to immerse yourself in the infectious energy and meet enthusiastic travellers keen to make friends and share stories. Whether you chose to take a drink from a street cocktail cart or visit one of the more upscale bars such as Silk, Bangkok has you now!

2)   Full Moon Party - Koh Phangan

This is one of the most famous beach parties in the world, and if you haven't heard about this party before then maybe you're not ready for it! Only joking! The full moon party is one hell of an extravaganza! This party is held at Haad Rin beach only once a month on the last full moon. This party can attract anywhere between 20,000 to 30,000 young excited travellers from all over the world to each event. The party starts at dusk and it doesn't take long for the beach to erupt into a complete dancing frenzy, lasting all the way into the night and through to the early hours of the morning, where you can catch a beautiful sunrise.

Photo Credit Mazu Travel /shutterstock.com

The DJs cater to all tastes in music from dance and techno to reggae and commercial hits. It is not all about the music either, with plenty of entertainment such as acrobats, fire juggling, and fireworks to amplify the excitement and keep you entertained. Participants often arrive in bright florescent clothes and faces painted to match the energetic and crazy atmosphere.

TOP TIP: Try and book accomodation in advance. Local hotels & hostels get booked up very quickly during this period.

3)   Ark Bar - Koh Samui

If you want to party on the beach that is less crazy than the full moon party, then the Ark Bar beach bar is the place for you. It is part of the Ark Bar resort, located in the heart of the beautiful Chaweng Beach. During the day, you have the option of getting involved in one of their regular pool parties, complete with pool bars, to grab your next drink. The DJs blast out dance and house music on a stage above the infinity pool that overlooks the golden sands and crystal water. With two beach front restaurants, there is a perfect opportunity to grab a bite to eat. Make sure to catch the breathtaking sunset and watch the party spill out on to the beach. This is where the tempo picks up and the Ark Bar comes to life.

Photo Credit somsak nitimongkolchai/shutterstock.com

With fire dancing, professional dances, and live music pumping, it's very similar to the Full Moon party, but on a much smaller scale. The age range here is a little more varied. The crowd is a mix of people in their late teens to mid-40s. Although the main genre of music here is house and dance, a variety of mixes can also be enjoyed. The party tends to start in the late afternoon depending on attendees, and ends around 2am the following morning.

Address:159/75, Moo 2, Chaweng Beach, Bophut, Koh Samui, 84320 Chaweng, Thailand

4)   Lebua State Tower Sky Bar – Bangkok

For a more sophisticated start to your night out, you cannot beat the rooftop bar at Lebua State Tower. The Sky Bar, also known as the "Hangover Bar" was featured in the second Hangover movie, making this bar famous. Set at around 820 feet in the sky, this bar is considered one of the world's highest rooftop bars. The most impressive thing about coming here is the sweeping views of Bangkok. You get the immense feeling of being on top of the world as you watch it pass by below you. Sunsets here are quite a spectacle, as well as the city lights at night that gently light up the Chao Phraya river and remind you of why Bangkok is called the city that never sleeps.

Photo Credit fokke baarssen /shutterstock.com

Music here is kept at a calmer level and is performed by live musicians, mainly playing Jazz. As for drinks, it is all about the cocktails. With talented mixologists at hand, you can indulge in anything from one of their signature sunset cocktails to seasonal cocktails. Being an up market venue, a smart casual dress code does apply and the drinks fall within a higher price range.

Address: 1055 Si Lom, Khwaeng Silom, Khet Bang Rak, Krung Thep Maha Nakhon 10500, Thailand

Opening times: 4pm to 1am daily (excluding Sundays 4pm to 12am)

5)   Bangla Road – Phuket

Known as the beating heart of the Phuket party scene, this 400-metre strip has much to offer. Coming to life at dusk, Bangla road is shut off to all vehicle traffic. It is illuminated by bright neon signs hanging from businesses on either side of the road. With the blur of bright lights and music pumping from every bar, the road almost merges in to one chaotic party. As well as the main strip, the night life here has spread out into many of the smaller adjoining streets. You will be spoiled with choices with open front bars, pubs, and clubs which are open late into the night. In addition, you will never be far from a restaurant or go go bar either.

Photo Credit Ruslan Kokarev /shutterstock.com

Street performers are also quite common and add fun entertainment to your night out. Be under no illusion though, Bangla Road is like Koh San Road on steroids. Local businesses have touts on the look out for any new face, often promising the world of whatever they think you want. Many of the clubs don't close until at least 4am, so take your time to explore. Politely decline persistent promoters and go where you want to.

Opening times: Upto 7 days a weeek depending on venue. Opening times range from 4pm to 2am and 9pm to 5am.

6)   RCA – Bangkok

Royal City Avenue (RCA) in Bangkok is a complete area dedicated to bars and night clubs. It is one of my favourite places to party in Thailand for many reasons. The variety of clubs and bars cater to every taste and genre of music. It's quite possible to experience an international DJ, a local band, and live concert all in the same night. RCA is much more up-market than places like Khao San or Bangla Road. Therefore, you don't need to worry about lady boys or go go girls trying to drag you into places. It is full of classy modern clubs with professional security, packed full of people who are simply out to socialise and dance the night away.

Photo Credit glazok90/shutterstock.com

Although more foreigners are now visiting RCA, it is a favourite for Thais and is the ideal place to see how Thais party. Be sure to take some form of ID and plan your transport as its location is not ideal for public transport such as buses or trains. All in all, with a trip to RCA you will discover multiple clubs with multiple rooms, playing multiple genres of music and attracting an array of different crowds. There is truly something for everyone and you really can't go wrong here.

Location: Royal City Avenue Bangkok (RCA)
Opening times: Upto 7 days a weeek depending on venue. Opening times range from 6pm to 2am and 9pm to 5am.

7)   Waterfall Party - Koh Phangan

Set within the lush tropical jungle of Ban Kai is the Waterfall Party. With large trees towering overhead, a back drop of large boulders, and a small waterfall, you have found a place in paradise to party. There is even a natural pool you can take a dip in. The setting here is best described as nothing but unique! The party is held two days before the full moon party and two days after, fitting for a great pre and after party. Pulling in up to 2000 people at each event, full efforts are put into making this a night for revellers to remember.

Photo Credit Geet Theerat /shutterstock.com

International DJs are common as the venue boasts one of Koh Phangan's largest sound systems, blasting out the very best of electro, techno, house, and more. Decorated with fluorescent art works, it's the perfect setting for fire dancers and acrobats to perform jaw dropping acts. There are also body paint artists on hand. You can find a variety of food stands here, including a BBQ.

8)   Blanco Boat Party - Koh Phi Phi

There is an array of options for places to party in Koh Phi Phi, but have you ever felt like you don't want to travel thousands of miles just to party and then miss out on things during the day? Well, with a Blanco boat party you can do both. Setting off in the afternoon, this is a daytime party which goes into the late evening. Blanco boasts the only party boat to have a live Dj. It also has an all-inclusive bar.

Photo Credit Tobi / Blanco Boat Party

As well as partying, you will actually get to enjoy and explore the local area and surrounding islands. The boat has a narrated tour while passing many historic landmarks and stopping on various islands. You will get the chance to take a dip and cool off, or simply chill on the beach. If you're not staying in Koh Phi Phi but are really keen on this idea, don't worry, Blanco offer services in Krabi and Koh Lanta. There are also many other companies at different beach resorts which offer similar services.

9)   Warm Up Café – Chiang Mai

When you mention the party scene in Thailand, most will quite naturally think of Bangkok or the Southern islands. However, the Warm Up Café in Chiang Mai is definitely an exception to this. Spread over three zones, this is one large buzzing party that often fills to capacity. You can expect to see live local bands playing indie and rock music, whilst the best DJs in Chiang Mai are blasting out EDM, house, and popular Music.

Photo Credit Pressmaster/shutterstock.com

The crowds here are mainly made up of Thai locals with a few in the know foreigners, all coming together to enjoy the electric atmosphere and forget the world for the night. It is particularly popular with Thai university students and gets very busy on weekends. You can pre-book tables, which is not a bad idea due to how busy it gets. Another good tip is to take your own spirits, which will incur a surcharge but work out cheaper in the long run. As with all Thai party scenes, drinking and eating go hand in hand. This place offers an alfresco style dining.

Address: 40 Nimman Hemin Road, Suthep Subdistrict, Mueang Chiang Mai District., Chiang Mai, Thailand.
Opening Times: Daily 7pm to 1am.

10)   So Pool Party – Bangkok

The top 10 party spots wouldn't be complete without the mention of a dedicated pool party. It is held on the last Saturday of every month at the Sofitel So Hotel. The crowd is mainly made up of local Thais, expats and in-the-know travellers. The setting of this pool party is what makes it one of the best. Located on the tenth floor, the open-air infinity pool looks out over the evergreen Lumpini Park. The city's skyline of high-rise buildings is impressive and needless to say, sunsets here are magical. In the evening, it transforms into a club with a dance floor by the pool. The pool party still continues with music pumping from underwater speakers. It is important to note, this is not an all-out all-night party as it runs for eight hours from 13.00hrs to 21.00hrs.

Photo Credit Rawpixel.com /shutterstock.com

Address: 2 N Sathon Rd, Khwaeng Bang Rak, Khet Bang Rak, Krung Thep Maha Nakhon 10500, Thailand.

CHAPTER 7 TOP 10 ALTERNATIVE ATTRACTIONS

1) Clean the beach Boot Camp – Phuket, Krabi and Koh Samui

If you love beaches, keeping fit, and are conscious of the natural environment, this is the perfect alternative activity for your stay in Thailand. Clean the beach boot camp runs FREE regular workouts on the beach in return for a small favour of getting your gloves on to clear up the beach after. Not only do you get a free workout in an idyllic setting, but it's a great way to meet like-minded travellers and locals whilst contributing to keeping Thailand beautiful and the natural environment safe and clean.

Photo Credit TravnikovStudio /shutterstock.com

2)   Sol Heng Tai Mansion Dive centre and living museum – Bangkok

The Sol Heng Tai Mansion is an ancient Chinese house built some 230 years ago, and is the last of its kind in Bangkok. Within its grounds hides a secret dive school. Set in the central court yard, the 4m pool is pretty impressive while the Mansion itself is rich with history. The descendants of the Sol clan actually still live here and entry is free to the public, although there is a fee for diving. If you're planning to head south for some diving, why not get some practice in whilst in Bangkok and enjoy some history all at the same time.

Photo Credit SuthiKait/shutterstock.com

Address: 282 Soi Wanit 2, Khwaeng Talat Noi, Khet Samphanthawong, Krung Thep Maha Nakhon 10100, Thailand
Opening times: Opens Tue.-Thurs. and Sun. open from 09-00-18.00 Fri.-Sat 09.00-21.00

3)   Gongs of the Phibun Mangsahan Village

If you want to witness a truly traditional and ancient art kept alive, a stop here will tick all the boxes. Located close to the Laos border is a small village called Phibun Mangsahan, which is famed for forging bronze gongs that are used in temples as musical instruments. They are all hand made by hammering and tempering the metal over a fire. The locals here are very friendly and more than happy to invite you into their workshops to show you how they are created. Although the village does attract some tourists, it still maintains a very rural and traditional way of life and is one of the last of its kind. You can find and purchase some genuine handcrafted products here, and also enjoy the views over the nearby rapids just downriver from the Mun River bridge.

Photo Credit amnat30/shutterstock.com

TOP TIP: Seek out a food vendor selling the local speciality, Vietnamese buns.

4)   Koh Tarutao Prison

Known as Thailand's very own Alcatraz, Koh Tarutao has a very dark history which includes around 3000 Thai prisoners being incarcerated between 1938 & 1949. Today, however, it is an island paradise and protected national park. It is untouched by chain hotels and commercial businesses. Although the jungle has swallowed up much of the prison's infrastructure, small traces can still be found. A small display of the remains and artfiacts can be found at the visitor centre in Ao Pante. There are no roads, very limited places to eat and stay, and due to its remote location, much fewer tourists make the visit here. However, having said that, it provides a quiet escape with the opportunity of enjoying the beautiful beaches, wildlife, and scenery of this tropical island.

Photo Credit fototrips /shutterstock.com

5)   Cycling in Bang Krachao – Bangkok

Bangkok, like any capital city, is best known for being fast paced and full of the hustle and bustle. Hidden just a short boat journey away is Bang Krachao. Protected by conservation laws, it is largely under developed and has a much slower pace of life. Paths and raised walk ways wind through the evergreen surroundings, allowing you to explore and experience a jungle-type adventure right in the heart of Bangkok. The best and most adventurous way to get around here is by bike though there are plenty of tour options to choose from. All in all, it is the ideal place to get away from the city's excitement and refresh your lungs whilst enjoying the natural environment at a leisurely pace.

Photo Credit TEERSAK KHUNRACH/shutterstock.com

6) Tree Top Dining – Soneva Kiri

With the variety of eating and dining options Thailand has to offer, the Tree Top dining experience has to be one of the most exciting ones. The dining area will be hoisted up 5 metres into the surrounding trees. You are then served by a waiter on a zip line going back and forth as you wish. This offers a unique experience with impressive views of the lush forest and stunning beach below you. The menu is pretty impressive too, as only locally sourced organic produce is used. Unfortunately, it is only really doable with a stay at the Soneva Kiri resort, which is featured in the top 10 beaches.

Photo Credit Paul Raeside/soneva brand centre

7) Rabeang Pasak Treehouse Resort

As I have mentioned, tree top dining offers a unique and alternative experience, but how about actually staying in a treehouse? It's like every child's dream come true! This family-run resort is located in a teakwood forest and has been designed to keep in harmony with its natural surroundings whilst providing comfort and good facilities to travellers. There are only 6 treehouses at this resort, making it fitting for anyone who wants to get away from over crowded tourist hot spots. If you ever wanted to get in touch with nature but aren't keen on a full camping experience, then Rabenag Pasak is the perfect choice.

8)   Yam Khang Massage

As most people are aware, Thailand is famous for its ancient practice of massage. However, very few are aware of the rare and ancient technique of Yam Khang. With the use of fire, heat, oils, and herbs, the body is massaged with only feet. This technique is somewhat different to the traditional Thai massage. This technique is said to have many health benefits and is used as a treatment for health complaints such as tendon, muscle, joint, and bone pain. One of the recommended places to experience this is in the village of Ban Rai Kong Khing in the Chiang Mai region. Not only are they one of the only villages to keep this technique alive, the village itself is said to be one of the best places in Thailand to experience the Thai Lanna culture.

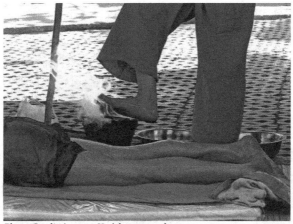

Photo Credit Aamam Ka/shutterstock.com

TOP TIP: This technique is very rare and hard to find. For your best chance, the most northern areas of Chiang Rai and Chiang Mai are the best bet.

9)   Koh Hingham - The cursed island of black pebbles.

This small uninhabited island is far from what you would expect to find in Thailand. It is full of black and white stones, which be warned, you should not take away as a souvenir. Thai mythology claims that anyone who does will forever be cursed by the God of Tarutao. The national park has even reported that they receive many packages from around the world returning stones which tourists have taken. With the island being small and uninhabited, there's not really much to do. However, a trip here is more about the adventure of trying to get a local to take you there, and enjoying the 20 minute or so boat ride. Once ashore you will find messages made from other travellers and small Chedi structures made by Thais. Some stones even have writing inscribed on them. The views here are pretty awesome too, and with no known local tour operators servicing this island you can expect it to be as fairly quiet and peaceful as a cursed island can be.

Photo Credit From sky to the Earth /shutterstock.com

10)   Bo Sang Umbrella Village

Bo Sang Village is located around 8km south east of Chiang Mai and is famous for producing umbrellas out of bamboo and sa paper. The local people are skilled artisans who have passed on their skills from generation to generation. You can witness the whole interesting process from start to finish. As well as umbrellas, they can also personalise your clothing, phone cases, and handbags with their skillful painting techniques. You can be sure that buying a souvenir from here will be unique. In the third week of January, they also hold an annual handicraft festival and competition. Although there are many tours from Chiang Mai, travelling here is not that difficult and may allow you more time and flexibility to explore the village itself.

Photo Credit Janon Stock /shutterstock.com

Address: 1014, Tambon Ton Pao, Amphoe San Kamphaeng, Chang Wat Chiang Mai 50130, Thailand
Opening times: 8.30am to 5pm Daily

CHAPTER 8 TOP 10 FOODS

I have had to break the theme of this chapter. I just couldnt pick 10! I am a foodie and it was just too much of a challenge, so I asked tFood and travel blogger the Roaming Cook to feature.

Check out our combined choices making up a total of 23 Thai foods which you must try!

1)   SPICY THAI SALAD / SOM TUM

Like salads and spicy food? Then Som Tum is a must try. Originally from Northeastern Thailand, this dish is widely available across Thailand. Its base ingredient is green papaya, which has tomato, peanuts, and green beans added to it. The secret to this dish tasting so great comes from the dressing. The dressing is made up of chilli, fresh lime juice, fish sauce, tamarind water, palm sugar, toasted peanuts, baby shrimp, and garlic which is all crushed together in a mortar and pestle. This creates an intense yet refreshing taste that will truly tingle your taste buds. It is best served as a side dish with cooked meat or sticky rice. Having said that, I've seen many people indulging in this dish by itself.

Photo Credit bonchan/shutterstock.com

2)   MANGO AND STICKY RICE/ KAO NIEW MA MUANG

Served as a dessert, it may sound strange that this dish includes rice, but please believe me it really works! This dish consists of the sweet and succulent Thai golden mango, paired with sticky rice, and flavoured in sweet coconut milk. This is quite a treat when served warm. Due to mangoes being readily available, this dish will be available throughout the year. Mango season in Thailand runs between April and June which would make it the best time of the year to indulge in this dish. This is definitely one dish that will taste its best in Thailand. Top tip for this one: Don't try this dish back home. Wait until you're in Thailand.

Photo Credit bochimsang12/shutterstock.com

3) PAD THAI

This is one of the most famous dishes in Thailand and is a must try. A little-known fact is that this dish was originally of Chinese origin, but over the years the Thais have truly enhanced its flavours and made it their own. Pad Thai is a stir fried rice noodle dish, commonly made with prawns, but you can choose from other meat or vegetarian options. The rice noodles are cooked in tamarind paste, fish sauce, eggs, brown sugar, garlic, bean sprouts, and topped with finely chopped peanuts. It is usually served with side garnishes of lime, chilli, and extra peanuts. This dish is beautifully balanced by sweet, sour, salty and bitter flavours. This isn't overly spicy.

Photo Credit wing f chen /shutterstock.com

TOP TIP: For some of Bangkoks best Pad Thai head to Thipsamai, but be prepared for long queues.

4)   CHICKEN AND RICE / KHAO MAN GAI

Khao Man Gai! One of Thailand's most under rated dishes and one of my personal favorites. The word essentially translates into "rice fat chicken" and is actually Hainanese in origin. This dish is quite popular with the Thai locals. The chickens are boiled whole and the broth is used both to cook the rice and to create a tasty side soup. The dish is served with a sweet, sour, and salty sauce which can really make or break the meal. I find this dish a great option if you want something that is simple, less fragrant and not spicy. Nothing goes to waste with this meal.

Photo Credit Thawarat Thangthawilap/shutterstock.com

TOP TIP: Find a vendor / resturant which only specialises in this dish. It will taste its best!

5)   SPICY SOUR SOUP / TOM YUM

This soup is packed full of flavour and, as the name suggests, it is a perfect combination of spicy, sour, sweet, and salty. Famously served with prawns (Tom Yum Goong), this fragrant soup is made from stock and a mixture of garlic, coriander, ginger, galangal, lime leaves, lemon grass, chillis, and shallots. Other meat and vegetarian options are available. Numerous versions of this dish can be found all over Thailand, which taste slightly different depending on the region. This is my go-to comfort food when feeling under the weather as it packs quite a punch!

Photo Credit Nachpapon Phantuvadee/shutterstock.com

6)   MINCED MEAT WITH CHILI AND BASIL / PAD KRA POW

This authentic street dish is quite simplistic in ingredients yet packed full of flavour. It is made from minced meat (commonly pork) that is stir fried with garlic, chilli, soy sauce, oyster sauce, Thai basil, and served with plain white rice topped with a fried egg. This is a meat lovers paradise with no vegetarian options available. As far as meat dishes go, this is quite a light dish, allowing you to indulge in other Thai dishes. Its popularity has awarded it a place on the menu in many restaurants all over Thailand.

Photo Credit Mama Belle and the kids/shutterstock.com

7)   STREET SATAY

When thinking of street satay in Thailand only one thing comes to mind: grilled meat on an open BBQ! And who doesn't love a good BBQ? Numerous meats ranging from chicken to pork are on offer. They also cater for the adventurous foodies with offerings such as intestines and liver. What makes this dish so delicious is the marinade, which is made from a blend of local spices and fresh ingredients. Pork satay marinade is usually made up of a blend of shallot, garlic, cumin, turmeric, ground coriander, lime, dark soy sauce, runny honey, and coconut milk. Cooking the meat on the grill usually mellows these flavours down, allowing only hints of these spices to be tasted. Satay is usually a snack/food on the go for me.

Photo Credit Manon van Os /shutterstock.com

TOP TIP: Don't forget to check out my tips on eating steet food in the top 10 tips chapter of this book.

8) . THAI CURRY

There is so much to be said about Thailand's authentic curries! Where do I start?! With many varieties on offer, I've had to generalise this. Most Thai curries are made from a fragrant and freshly made curry paste. This curry paste usually consists of chilli, garlic, shrimp, and onions or shallots. This paste forms the base of the dish and is usually mixed in with coconut milk and/or water. A range of meats and vegetables are added to the curry.

These curries range from a variety of spice levels, allowing you to choose based on personal preferences. My personal favourites are green chicken and lamb massaman curries.

Photo Credit Kate Sun/shutterstock.com

If this still isnt enough information for you dont worry the Roaming Cook has great choices, which he breaks down later in the chapter.

9) STEAMED FISH / PLAH KAH PUNG NEUNG MANOW

This dish is made using a whole fish, commonly a snapper or bass, that is topped with a marinade made from freshly chopped garlic, lime leaves, coriander, and lime juice. It is then steamed and served whole with a serving of rice. The end dish is aromatic with a tangy, sweet taste. The way in which the fish is cooked ensures the meat is tender and succulent. Even those who aren't overly keen on fish will enjoy this dish, as the taste is not overly fishy. Don't let the sight of a whole fish put you off either, you only have to eat what parts of it you choose!

Photo Credit buengza/shutterstock.com

10)   JIM JUM

"Jim Jum" essentially translates to Thai hot pot. Hot pots usually consist of a range of uncooked meats, vegetables, and noodles that will be cooked by yourself in a broth. It provides a great dining experience usually enjoyed with family or friends.

In Thailand, you are provided with a flavoursome, aromatic pork broth that is served in a small clay pot on a bed of charcoal, with a choice of your selected ingredients. The end result is usually an authentic, hearty soup noodle dish. This dish is included in my top picks not just because it's a nice meal to eat, but also because it's a fun and social experience to have.

Photo Credit Oilly.Ar/shutterstock.com

TOP TIP: The food court at Chiang rai night Bazzar has many vendors who specialise in this dish.

11)   GANG JUED

Gang Jued is a soup type dish which is clear in colour and packed full of goodness. Whilst it has many tasty ingredients, it has more of a delicate taste. It can be a nice break from all the more aromatic and spicy Thai dishes. A fresh and crisp flavour is created using a combination of glass noodles, carrots, cabbage, minced pork, tofu, and a dressing of parsley or coriander. Another great thing about this dish is that it really compliments so many other dishes, although you could have this as a light meal on its own if you choose. Healthy, fresh tasting, and mild, you can't go wrong with Gang Jued.

Photo Credit Jesse33/shutterstock.com

12)   Kao Na Phet

Time for a duck dish! Not just any, but an Asian roasted duck!

Whatever you do with these top picks, make sure you try some roasted duck. It is considered a speciality across Southeast Asia, and Thailand is no exception. Duck, being fattier than chicken, has a more distinctive taste. Being cooked in Thailand, this is more than simply putting a duck in the oven and roasting it! It is often marinated with a soy, ginger, and honey marinade and coated throughout the cooking process with the hot duck stock. Once complete, it is served on a bed of jasmine rice, with a sauce made from the duck stock and a side duck soup to compliment your eating experience. Absolutely mouth-watering!

Photo Credit Hassel Sinar /shutterstock.com

13)   THAI PANCAKE / ROTI

Found at almost any night market, the Thai pancake is a perfect sweet snack or dessert. You are probably thinking, "how many ways are there to cook a pancake?" The way they work the pastry is an art in itself and fun to watch. This method originates from India but the Thais have, of course, put their touch to it and made it their own. Using a large hot plate coated with butter, the batter is thinly spread across. As the bottom layer becomes cooked and crisp, the pastry is filled with any fruit of your choice and/or chocolate spread. It is then folded up into a smaller parcel, coated with a sprinkle of sugar and condensed milk, and chopped into smaller squares for ease of eating. It will always be cooked on the spot, adding to the freshness. If you are not keen on having too many fillings, it is just as tasty without.

Photo Credit 365dayjsustthewayiam/shutterstock.com

14) Khao Soi - Northern Thai Curry Noodles (The Roaming Cook)

Northern Thailand's most famous dish, this coconut-based curry is said to have been adapted from the Burmese dish, *Khow suey.* Thai Khao Soi consists of egg noodles in an Indian spiced coconut curry broth topped with crispy, fried egg noodles and served with fresh shallots, pickled cabbage and roasted chilli oil (prik garian). If you're looking for a taste of regional northern Thailand, this is the one.

15) Sai Ua - Chiang Mai Sausage (The Roaming Cook)

Perhaps the world's best sausage, Sai Ua is shaped in a coil like a traditional English Cumberland Sausage. However, that is where the similarities end! This Chiang Mai sausage just screams Thailand as soon as you take a bite. Chilli, lemongrass, lime leaves, garlic, and galangal. All the classic flavours you associate with Thai food in one fatty, meaty bite.

16) Khanom Jeen Nam Ngiow - Northern Thai Tomato Stew with Fresh Rice Noodles. (The Roaming Cook)

Sometimes referred to as 'Thai Bolognese' due to the fact that it's made up of minced meat in a tomato broth, this is a dish that's extremely foreigner friendly (with the possible exception of the chunks of congealed pork blood). It contains an interesting ingredient that you won't find in any other dish called dok ngiow, the dried flower from the red cotton tree, and also includes pork ribs and minced pork.

17) Khao Kha Moo - Thai Pork Leg Stew (The Roaming Cook)

Originating in southern China, Khao Kha Moo, or pork leg stew, is my ultimate Thai comfort food. I eat it at least once a week, if not more. This is a slow cooked pork leg, simmered in a five-spice infused broth for hours until it's falling off the bone. Served on top of steamed jasmine rice with boiled eggs, which take on the flavour of the meaty stock. Khao Kha Moo is a dish found on literally every street corner in Bangkok.

18) Bamee Kieow Moo Daeng - Egg Noodles with Wontons and BBQ Pork (The Roaming Cook)

Bamee Kieow Moo Daeng, or egg noodles with wontons and BBQ pork, has to be in the top five most eaten dishes in Thailand. Seriously, it's everywhere! You can have it **nam** (with soup) or **haeng** (dry). Personally, I like to get mine dry with a bowl of soup on the side. You can dress your noodles up to suit your own taste with soy, fish sauce, sugar, and chilli vinegar, which are always found wherever this dish is served.

19) Kua Khling Moo - Dry Southern Curry Stir Fry (The Roaming Cook)

This Southern Thai stir fried, dry, minced meat curry has the reputation for being viciously hot. It is usually made with minced pork, but you can also find it with beef, chicken, and sometimes even deer! The base paste is a mixture of lemongrass, turmeric, lime leaves, shallot, shrimp paste, and chilli...a LOT of chilli! If you're looking to try something 'Thai Spicy,' look no further.

20) Khanom Jeen Nam Ya - Coconut Fish Curry with Fresh Rice Noodles (The Roaming Cook)

This is very high on the list for me. This is a coconut-based fish curry where the main flavour comes from Krachai, or fingerroot, which is a ginger like rhizome with a slightly medicinal taste. It happens to go amazingly well with fish. It's served with an array of fresh herbs and vegetables that really freshen things up. This street classic can be found in every province of Thailand and is a real firm favourite with locals for breakfast.

21) Gaeng Som Khai Jeow Cha Om - Spicy Sour Orange Curry with Acacia Omelette (The Roaming Cook)

Gaeng Som refers to the 'curry,' which is actually a sour, hot soup with prawns and different vegetables that vary depending on whether you are getting it in Central or Southern Thailand; anything from cauliflower to watermelon rind is used. The Khai Jeow Cha Om is a Thai fried omelette made from the fern like plant, Cha Om, and is the perfect accompaniment to the spicy soup broth.

22) Pad Sataw Moo Koong - Stir Fried Prawns with Pork and Stink Beans (The Roaming Cook)

Sataw, or stink beans, grow abundantly in the south of Thailand, so it's no surprise that they are found in an array of spicy Southern Thai dishes. My favourite of these is Pad Sataw Moo Koong. Fresh prawns and pork are stir fried with the stink beans and the same southern curry paste as Kua Khling, then topped with shredded kaffir lime leaves.

23) Kuay Tiow Kua Gai - Fried Flat Rice Noodles with Chicken (The Roaming Cook)

Kuay Tiow means noodles in Thai, Kua is to fry in a wok until dry, and Gai is chicken. The name literally translates to dry fried chicken noodles and that pretty much sums them up. Unlike the more famous cousins, pad Thai and pad see-ew, there is no special sauce used in Kuay Teow Kua Gai. All the flavour comes from being cooked over coals at an insanely high heat in pork fat with a little soy sauce and finished with spring onions and egg. The flat, wide rice noodles char and blister and you end up with something resembling a noodle omelette.

CHAPTER 9 TOP 10 THAI WORDS / SENTENCES

1)   Ka and Krap

This is an easy one but also very important! You use either the word Ka or Krap to end your sentence. Ka if you are female and Krap if you are male, it's that easy! It is the polite way of speaking to someone in Thailand.

2)   Sawadee Krap / Ka = Hello

Essentially translating into "hello," these words are best used when greeting someone. Give it a go, don't be scared!

3)   Sabidee mai Krap / Ka = How are you?

You can use these words when you first meet someone and after saying hello. It would then translate into "Hello, how are you?". You would need to say, "sawadee ka, sabidee mai ka?" If you are ever asked, "sabidee mai ka," you can simply reply with "sabidee ka."

4)   Kop khun krap / Ka = Thank you

This is another easy word to pick up, but one that will go a long way. "Thank you" in Thai is "Kop khun krap / ka." If you want to be really cultural don't forget to smile and put your hands together in a wai. Again remember to end your sentence with "krap" for men and end it with "ka" for women.

5)   Kor tod na krap / ka = Sorry or excuse me

This word can be used to say both excuse me or sorry. "kor tod na krap / ka." If you bumped into someone by accident you could say "Kor tod na krap" (sorry)! Or if you wanted to get a waiter or waitress' attention you could also say "ka tod na krap" (excuse me).

6)   Mai ao krap / Ka = No thank you or I don't want it

This short sentence often helps keep eager street venders and unwanted tuk tuks away. When asked "tuk tuk come get in my tuk tuk" if you don't need this service at the time, simply reply with "mai ow karp," meaning I don't want it/need it. You will often notice the difference rather than saying it in English.

7)   Ped Ka / Krap = Spicy

This word will assist you when eating all the great food Thailand has to offer. The word "spicy" in Thai is pronounced "Ped". If you are not a massive fan of spicy food you can say, "mai ow ped krap." If you like spicy food you can say, "pom chob ped krap," meaning "I like spicy."

8)   Chokdee Krap / Ka = Good luck

You may hear Thais saying this when parting or saying farewell! Chokdee in simple translation is good luck, and a kind thing to say in Thailand. Remember to end it with ka if female and karp if male. Chokdee na krap / good luck to you all.

9)   Tao-Rai-KA / Krap = HOW MUCH

This word translates to "how much?" For the cost of an item in a shop or market, try using this in markets, mixing it up with your other Thai words like "Sawasdee ka, Sabidee Mai ka Ta-roi-ka" (Hello, how are you? How much is this?). It may just help you get a better price.

10)   Pom ja pai or Chan ja pai = I'm going to

Another great language tip to help you get about, Pom Ja Pai for men Chan Ja Pai for women translates to "I'm going to…" This is a good sentence to learn and can be used when getting into taxis and tuk tuks, or other modes of transport. You can say Pom ja pai MBK or Pom ja pai Airport, mixing it with English. I've always found mixing in a bit of Thai when getting in taxis or tuk tuks can often help you get a better price. With all the above tips you can now say, "Sawasdee Karp / Ka, sabidee mai Karp/ka pom ja pai MBK."

CHAPTER 10 TOP 10 TIPS FOR TRAVELLING /
VISITING THAILAND

Street Food Tips

One of the things Thailand is most famous for is its street food, and for good reason! However, occasionally the odd horror story pops up. Follow these basic tips to make sure you enjoy the yummy selection of street food available safely.

1)   Ask for hot, freshly cooked food. Don't be shy, most vendors will be happy to do this for you if requested.

2)   Look for a popular vendor which has both Thais and foreigners alike lining up to get served!

3)   Aim to eat foods that are stir fried at a really high heat or even deep fat fried, which will kill bacteria and taste really good.

4)   Do your research! There are certain street vendors out there that are well known for producing quality and amazingly tasty dishes. So much so, they make their mark on such websites as TripAdvisor.

5)   Try to find somewhere that cooks one type of food or just a few options as this avoids any cross-contamination.

6)   Take hand sanitizer with you. Many people get ill not because of the food that they have eaten but because of what they have touched before eating street food.

7)   Enjoy, eat lots, and try something new!

Visiting Temples (wat) in Thailand

1)   Make sure you arrive wearing the appropriate clothes. This will save you time and money! Women are expected to cover all skin from the neck down. Hands and feet are allowed to be out, however. Although men are often let in with shorts and t-shirts, but it is best to cover up out of respect.

2)   Please do not think the above tip is sexist. One of the reasons that women are asked to cover up more is because part of a Buddhist monks' practice is to give up all worldly temptations. Exposing more skin could be conveyed as a distraction. Buddhists and Thais are far from sexist.

3)   Keeping the last tip in mind, women should not touch monks at all, not even their clothing.

4)   Take your shoes off before entering any place of worship and certain temple grounds. You will often see signs or others doing this, so please follow suit.

5)   Do not point your feet at any Buddha statues, pictures or symbols as this is very disrespectful.

6)   Remember, temples are meant as a place of peace and worship, so if you are arriving as a tourist, please give priority and respect to those who have come for these reasons.

7)   As part of the monks' practice, they will not eat after noon, so please try not to eat around them after this point in the day.

8)   Do not touch any Buddha statues or images; it is even considered bad to point.

9)   Be careful with taking photos. It is understandable that you are on holiday and may be impressed and excited, but please take care with the type of photos you decide to take. Selfies, silly faces, and positions will be very frowned upon, and could even get you arrested.

10)   If someone approaches you saying the temple is closed, please go to the entrance and find out for yourself.

11)   Don't be surprised if you are charged more than Thai people. This is normal in many temples as you are seen as a tourist and Thais are seen as people going there to make merit and pray.

Using your Mobile / Cell phone in Thailand

1)   Get your current Phone / cell unlocked before you reach Thailand, or buy a second-hand unlocked one.

2)   If flying into Bangkok you will be able to pick up a sim card pretty much straight after you get out of customs, right in the airport.

3)   Don't be put off by long ques outside the sim kiosks, they often move quickly and will be worth the wait if you want a means of communication from the get-go!

4)   If you are in a rush, don't worry, you can easily pick up sim cards all around Thailand either in 7/11 convenient stores or shopping malls.

5)   There will be options from the following service providers: DTAC, True, and AIS. They are all similar in value, but make sure to check out what package is right for you. I would always choose the option with the best internet deals. This package often lasts longer when using apps such as Whatsapp, Line, or Skype compared with actual minutes and talk time.

6)   If you arc travelling with more than one person or as a group it is recommended that you get a few sims and phones set up as it will be cheaper in the long run.

7)   Now that you're all set up, don't forget to share some of your beautiful moments on social media, and make everyone back at home jealous.

Monsoon Season Tips / Ideas

Monsoon Season in Thailand runs from around June to October. Even when it rains in Thailand, it will still be warm. Often the rain will not last all day. Flurries of short, heavy showers are common. However, all is not lost. Here is my list of things to do in case of bad weather:

1) Thai massage

2) Cooking classes

3) Yoga

4) Fruit carving lessons

5) Watch Muay Thai (kick boxing)

6) Give the above a go yourself and train in Muay Thai

7) Complete spa day

8) Go to a shopping mall

9) Enjoy having nothing to do for once and have a lazy day in your hotel.

10) Remember that the rain will often pass as quick as it comes, but please take care and keep an eye on all forecasts and be aware of your surroundings.

Riding Tuk Tuks

1)   Agree a price before you get in or on.

2)   Do not accept a discounted fair on the condition of you stopping at a "friends shop" as you will be expected to buy something. Unless you really are after a new suit and that's the type of shop, then by all means go ahead!

3)   Don't Travel alone!

4)   If you're travelling alone and you get a chatty driver, which often happens (who is most likely genuine), always mention you are on your way to meet Thai friends! This will deter any dishonest behaviour!

5)   Keep all limbs in the Tuk Tuk at all times, especially in places like Bangkok. The traffic can get heavily congested yet be moving at speed.

6)   Keep all loose valuable items hidden or well secured to prevent any grab and runs by motorcyclists.

7)   Try and use Tuk Tuks in less congested areas/towns as this will ensure you get the most out of the open-air experience. Getting stuck in traffic is often unpleasant as the atmosphere can get very hot and sticky with thick motor fumes.

8)   ENJOY the experience, it is a must! The warm air rushing past you, the noise of the rumbling engine beneath and the bright colours of the Tuk Tuk and surroundings will truly make you feel alive!

Renting a Jet ski in Thailand

Whilst most water sport vendors are there to make a good and honest income, you may still come across the occasional scammer who will try and charge you for 'damages' you did not cause. See my top tips below on how to avoid being caught out.

1)   Do not give your passport or anything of high value as a deposit or collateral for renting a jet ski!

2)   Make sure you check out the jet ski for any original damage before you take it out on the water. If you find anything, politely point it out and if possible take a photo on your phone for record's sake.

3)   Stay calm if any disputes come to light. In Thailand, getting angry in public can make you the guiltier one, even if you are not! Plus, to think clearly you need to be calm.

4)   Go to a busy vendor which plenty of people are using. You may have to wait a little longer but it will be worth it. Those who are busier are normally more established, are happy giving a good service, and receiving regular income.

5)   Be careful when out on the water. Stay away from other jet skis, boats, and busier areas. Try not to turn into James Bond and do silly tricks.

6)   Be careful of wildlife and keep away from reefs, rocks, and shallow waters.

7)   If you know where you're heading, do your research first and check out such sites as TripAdvisor.

8)   Enjoy the experience, don't let these tips worry you. Simply keep the above in mind and go for it.

Exchanging your currency for Thai baht!

1)   It really is simple. Wait to exchange the bulk of your money in Thailand, as 9 times out of 10 you will get a better rate than what is offered to you back home. If you're exchanging a fair amount, then this really is worth the wait.

2)   Best rates are available at the "Super Rich" branch at Suvarnabhumi airport, Bangkok. Otherwise, make sure to wait until you leave your arrival airport as the rates will be slightly better!

3)   Keep some emergency cash funds to exchange if needed. This will avoid unnecessary bank charges from using your bank/credit card abroad.

4)   Don't forget to exchange a small amount back home. This will keep you going until you reach a money exchange.

5)   Make sure that the currency you bring to Thailand is in good condition, i.e. no pen marks, rips/tears as it may be rejected.

6)   As mentioned, "Super Rich" Bank is currently trending as the best exchange rate. These are located in numerous areas but not all towns and provinces.

7)   If you are travelling for a longer period of time or have a large amount of cash, and feel a bit un-easy about carrying this around. You can always opt for a travel card such as Caxton or Sterling.

8)   Taking in to account point 7, remember many places such as night markets and small street vendors will not accept card. It's always a good idea to keep a cash on you even if you opt for a travel card option. You will also be charged a withdrawal fee at any ATM in Thailand, regardless of the type of card you have.

Renting a scooter

1)   The first tip would be to reconsider renting a scooter. Thailand has the worst record in the world for road accident fatalities. However, if you really are adamant on renting a scooter, follow my tips below.

2)   Make sure you are an experienced scooter/motor bike rider. If you are not, please again reconsider.

3)   Make sure you have the correct licence and insurance coverage. Request that the hire company provides documentation to clarify this in case you are stopped by the police or involved in an accident.

4)   An obvious one: Make sure you wear a helmet! Yes, it is hot and yes you will see many people riding around without wearing one BUT, it could potentially save your life. Make sure that the helmet you rent also fits correctly and go for the option which presents the most protection.

5)   Wear long clothes for protection even if it is hot. Choose suitable foot wear. Sandals/sliders are not recommended.

6)   Try and rent your scooter/bike in areas with less traffic.

7)   Like the jet ski scam, this can also happen with a scooter. Apply our tips on renting a jet ski to renting a scooter.

8)   Check that the scooter/bike is in good working order. Ask for a quick test drive if possible.

Avoiding Mosquito bites

Unfortunately, in countries such as Thailand, the hot and humid conditions make it inevitable to be bitten by mosquitos. Please follow my tips on how to minimise this.

1)   Start with most obvious, use mosquito repellent. I recommend 'Deet' repellent as it works the best.

2)   In general, try and wear more neutral/earth colours such as khaki. Bright clothes are much more likely to attract mosquitos.

3)   Keep clean and hygienic (I'm sure you will). Mosquitos are attracted to body sweat and body odour.

4)   Keeping the above tip in mind, don't got over board in smelling too nice. Mosquitos, particularly breading females, feed on nectar from flowers. Anything that is too sweet in scent could easily attract unwanted attention. This could include fragrances from body lotion, flower soaps, and even your favourite perfume.

5)   If your accommodation provides mosquito nets for your bed, use them. I personally never have, but it's logical that this will help.

6)   Try and keep your skin covered as practically as possible.

7)   Gecko Lizards (JING JOG in Thai) have been observed to eat up to several insects a minute, including mosquitos. So, if you find any of these little creatures in or around your room, leave them be. They will do more good than harm.

8) Mosquito coils can work quite well in outside areas.

9)   Mosquitos tend to become a lot more active and feed more as dusk approaches. Keep this in mind and give the above tips some extra thought when it does.

General cultural tips

This next list is to help assist you with some of the simple do's and don'ts which fall in line with Thai Culture and some laws.

1)   DON'T touch people's heads as this is seen as disrespectful.

2)   DON'T talk bad about the Royal Family as even opinions can get you into trouble. The Thai Royal Family are loved, respected, and adored. Thailand has the 'lese majeste' rule, which means that if you commit disrespectful acts toward the King or royal family, you could be imprisoned.

3)   Don't be offended by questions about age, marital status, or what you do for a living.

4)   Don't take Buddha statues, images, or even memorabilia out of the country. It is technically illegal to remove a Buddha statue/images out of the country, unless special permissions have been given. This may be tempting and confusing due to the amount of vendors trying to sell such items.

5)   Don't vape or use E-cigarettes. The use of E-cigarettes throughout the world has risen incredibly in the past 5 years, but unfortunately, they are illegal in Thailand. Many people are still very unaware of this. I have seen many people using them in public, but it is not worth the risk of being arrested for vaping on holiday.

6)   Don't place your feet on the table while sitting, don't point to anything with your feet, and don't touch anybody with your feet.

7)   Do eat with a spoon. Use the fork to load food onto the spoon. Ok, so you won't get chased out of Thailand for this one, but it is quite a cultural thing, never the less.

8)   Do lower your body slightly when passing between or in front of people.
9)   Do try and speak some basic Thai. This will go a long way, help with socialising, and even getting a better price at markets/shops. If you haven't already, check out our top 10 language tips in chapter 9.

FAQ THAILAND

TRANSPORT IN THAILAND

Taxis - In cities such as Bangkok, Taxis should be on a meter. Occasionally this does not happen; just be polite and decline any taxi driver who refuses to use the meter. You will find another taxi soon enough. In major cities such as Bangkok and Chaing Mai they do have the app called "Grab," this is basically the equivalent of Uber. You can find very reasonable fares with this service, and the price is set before you choose your driver.

Trains - You can easily buy tickets for any train journey at a Thai Train station. For long distance journeys, it is best advised that you book in advance. Unfortunately, the State Railways of Thailand website, is not the most modern or user friendly. As an alternative you can use 12Go Asia, where you can book with ease online.

MRT and BTS Bangkok - The MRT in Bangkok is very similar to that of the underground in London or the metro in New York. The Bangkok sky train (BTS) is a network of rail links that has been constructed above the roads and some buildings. Both are a great way of beating Bangkok's traffic, but like most public transport, can get very busy during rush hour.

Tuk Tuks - These 3 wheeled open sided vehicles can be quite fun to ride in! However, They are normally more expensive than a metered Taxi and you don't get any air-con.

Bus - If you are looking to travel long distance journeys by bus, make sure you use reputable companies such as Nakhon Chai Air and the Green Bus Company. These companies service a wide range of destinations and also provide overnight services. Travelling by bus in Thailand can be very cheap, but it is also one of the slowest forms of transport.

Airlines and Airports - All major cities and tourist destinations such as Bangkok, Chiang Mai, Chiaing Rai, Phuket, Koh Samui, Surat Thani, Krabi are serviced by domestic flights and international flights. There are also many smaller airports across Thailand that are serviced by domestic flights. Using this method of transport is relatively cheap and quick, what could be an over night train from Bangkok to Chiang Mai, would be done in not much more than and hours flight time by plane. Songthew -These are converted pick up trucks which have been kitted out with two rows of seats along the back of the vehicle. They are a popular form of public transport across most of Thailand. They are very reasonably priced when sharing with other passengers, although it is possible to rent them out privately.

Ferry Services - For travel between coastal towns and cities, a ferry service can serve as a convenient and reasonably priced option. You can often by tickets on the day of travel, or if you wish to book in advance you can do this online via 12Go Asia.

Long tail Boats - These iconic boats have become a popular way of exploring the Southern waters and Islands of Thailand. Its important to note that they are best suited to being used in shore and around islands rather than across open water and deeps seas. You can either share with other passengers or rent privately. Make sure a life jacket is provided.

VISAS FOR TOURISTS

Citizens arriving from ASEAN or Western countries, including most European, Commonwealth, and North American are entitled to a 30 day tourist visa on arrival. You must hold a passport with a minimum 6 months validity and proof of onward travel.
For extended visits you must go to an immigration office in Thailand or a consulate / embassy outside of Thailand. Visa runs are common; this is when travellers want to extend for another 30 days, and will leave Thailand travelling to one of its bordering countries. This will enable another visa on arrival when returning.
It's important to note that Visa policies are constantly evolving and are always subject to change. For the most up to date information please check at www.mfa.go.th

VACCINATIONS

Currently there are no mandatory vaccinations for persons travelling from the UK, Europe and Northern America to Thailand. This is unless they have previously visited a country where yellow fever is present. However, the recommended vaccines are as follows:
Cholera, Hepatitis A, Hepatitis B, Japanese Encephalitis, Rabies, Tuberculosis (TB) and Typhoid.
It is important to note that you should always seek professional medical advice to address individual requirements. In addition, you should always check for the most up to date information, in case of any updates or changes. You can do this via the National Travel Health Network and Centre on the TravelHealthPro Website.

THAI CURRENCY -The Currency used in Thailand is the the Thai Baht.

CASH: As with many other countries cash is king, it is advised you exchange your money in Thailand to ensure you get the best rate. The super rich branch always provides the best exchange rate. The other advantage of using cash / Thai Baht is that there are many places such as night markets and food stalls which will not have card payment facilities. In case you do not have time straight away or for any unforeseen circumstances, it is always a good idea to exchange enough money before you depart. This will keep you going when you arrive in Thailand.

ATM AND CARD PAYMENTS: You will find many ATM machines and shops which except card payments across Thailand. These will all incur withdrawal fees and/or foreign currency fees. As mentioned above you will also find that many places do not expect card payments such as markets, food stalls, and street vendors. Remember if you are going use a bank card, you must notify your issuing bank of its use in Thailand. This will stop it from getting blocked. It's always a good idea to do this as a back up even if you do not intend to use it.

TRAVELLERS CHEQUES: The majority of Banks in Thailand expect travellers cheques. You can often get a slightly better exchange rate, but you will be charged a fee per each traveller cheques, so this can sometimes cancel out any gains. You must also remember to bring your passport as proof of ID.

WHAT TO BRING

It's safe to say you can find pretty much find anything you need in Thailand. However, the below list provides you with the essentials to bring or purchase before you arrive.

Mosquito repellent - Mosquitos won't wait for you to get to the nearest pharmacy. Often brand names, if you can find them, will cost just as much or more than back in your home country.

Light cotton or linen clothing - Clothing made from these materials are best suited to the tropical climate. Shorts, vests, and T-shirts are perfect but make sure you take longer clothing for visits to religious places such as Temples. When entering Temples you will be required to cover up your legs and arms.

Formal / smart casual clothing - Some roof top bars and up market night clubs have a smart casual dress code. It's worth taking at least one outfit of this sort including footwear.

Jumper or light jacket - This is for journeys on transport where the air-con may catch you out.

A Photo copy of official documents - This can range from anything from a passport to ID and is just a precaution for the worst-case scenario of having something lost or stolen.

Sun Lotion - Brand names in Thailand can cost just as much and if not more than in your home country.

Plug adaptor - Thailand uses 220Vc Electricity. This means the majority of sockets will only receive a two prong plug.

TRAVEL INSURANCE

There is no legal requirement to have travel insurance when entering Thailand. However, is it strongly recommended that you do! There is no such thing as free medical health care in Thailand. If you require any medical assistance you will need to pay for it, and depending on what assistance you will need it can be very expensive. Most travel insurance will cover you for medical assistance and additional items, such as lost luggage, cancellations, and stolen or damaged goods.

BOOKING TOURS

Booking tours in Thailand couldn't be easier. Most hotels and accommodation will have either have a dedicated tour desk or at least, information and contacts for assisting you. You will also come across many tourist information desks across Thailand, where you can book tours and activities. If you are the type that likes to plan ahead, you can book online via such sites as Klook and Tripadvisor links. Although normally reasonably priced, this method won't allow you to barter on price. But it does give you the added benefit of being able to research ahead and check out reviews.

WEATHER IN THAILAND

The weather in Thailand is led by three main seasons. Hot season, cool season, and wet season. Generally speaking the hot season runs from February/March to May/June, where temperatures in some areas can surpass 40 Celsius. The wet season runs from June to October and the cool season runs from November to February. However, the tropical monsoon climate of Thailand brings varied weather to various regions throughout the year. Each region can slightly differ from one another. Below is information on the weather in each of the different regions.

WEATHER IN NORTHEASTER THAILAND

November to March
These months are classed as the cool season. Rain is rare and temperatures whilst warm are much more bearable, compared to the rest of the year. In terms of comfortable weather this is the best time of the year to visit.

March to May
These months are classed as the hot season. Temperatures often soar well into the high 30s and remain there. Any rain that may happen is normally quite welcome.

June to October
These months are classed as the wet season, but don't panic the rain will often only last around an hour in the afternoon or evening. The rains during this season bring out the most beautiful landscapes and attractions. The forests and fields are a lush green and lakes and waterfalls become full and powerful.

WEATHER IN NORTHERN THAILAND

November to January
These months are in Thailand's "winter" and cool season. Day time temperatures will sit around 20° to 23°c, whilst at night time have been known to dip very close to freezing, in certain places.

March to May

These months are classed as the hot season, where it is not uncommon for day time temperatures to exceed 40°c. Its is important to note this is also the burning season in some provinces. Burning season is where local farming communities cut down their crops and burn off the fields. This can cause the air to smell and create a smokey scent and haze, which often will linger until the first rains.

June to October
These months see the rainy season set in. However, the rain will often pass as quick as it comes. Outdoor activities such as hiking may become more difficult and all such activities should be carefully planned.

WEATHER IN CENTRAL THAILAND AND BANGKOK

February to June
These months bring the hot season temperatures often hit the high 30s. The months of March and April can be particularly hot.

June to October
These months bring the rainy season. In the months of August, September and October heavy down pours and flooding are not uncommon.

October to January
These months see the cool season or "cooler" season with much less rain from around November / December.

WEATHER IN SOUTHERN THAILAND

The weather in the Southern regions on Thailand is split by two main seasons, The dry season and wet season. However, these seasons effect the southeast coast and southwest coast at different times.
The southwest coast will experience its dry season from November to March and its wet season from around April / May to October. With heaviest rains normally falling between September and October.
The southeast coast will experience its dry season from January to May and its wet season from around June to December.

USEFUL TELEPHONE NUMBERS

Tourism Authority of Thailand (TAT) 1672

Tourist Police 1155 (languages - English, German and French)

Tourist Service desk 1672

Telephone Directory Assistance 1133

Highway Police 1193

Police: 191

Ambulance: 1554

Fire: 199

Immigration Bureau: +66 (0)2 287 3101 to 10

Suvarnabhumi International Airport +66 (0)2 132 1888

Bangkok Taxi Call Center 1681, 1661, +66 (0)2 424 2222

Bangkok Hospital emergency room: +66 (0)2 310 3102

CONCLUSION

Thanks for choosing the Everything Thai Top Tens of Thailand Guide book! I hope you have enjoyed reading all the information that I provided.

It has been no easy task! For topics such as Temples, there are around 33,000 in Thailand, and for beaches there are over 2,000 miles of coastline.

The concept of the book was to find a little something for everyone and save you the hard work. Even if you only take a few of my reccomendations you will not be dissapointed. The book is only an introduction to Thailand and I intend to keep on going with peeling back this beautiful country's infinite layers.

To stay updated and get more tips and tricks to Thailand, make sure to follow my blog at www.everythingthai.co.uk or check out the Everything Thai Facebook page. I cover everything from reviews and featured content to news and recommendations. Showcasing the very best of Thailand and everything Thai.

You can even subscribe to the mailing list to get free exclusive information using the below link.
https://www.everythingthai.co.uk/subscribe.html

In addition to the above I would love any feed back you may have on the book. You can do this my using the contact page on the Everything Thai website https://www.everythingthai.co.uk/contact-everything-thai.html

Oh, one more thing: Please be sure to check out the "about my sponsor" page. To see who contrubuted to making this book happen, you can also find a little more out about Thailand and the amazing service they offer.

ABOUT MY SPONSOR

Draco Charters is a yacht charter company based on Thailand's largest island, Phuket. The island is well known for year-round tourism from various markets that build in strength, year-on-year. Avoid the crowded speed boat tours and join them on a luxury sailing yacht, ensuring you make it a holiday to remember.

As a yacht broker, they offer a collection of boats that range from mono hulls, sailing yacht, catamarans, motor yachts and superyachts. With its gently curving coastline, craggy limestone islands, colorful marine parks and untouched sandy coves, it won't take you long to realise why exploring using a luxury charter is one of the best ways to see the Pearl of the Andaman.

Choose from their wide range of private yacht charters and discover the tropical bliss where you'll find more than 130 islands to explore. Wind your way through mysterious, emerald waters, drop anchor off deserted beaches and moorings in completely untouched and undeveloped fishing villages still steeped in ancient cultures.

For world-class diving and snorkeling, excellent sport fishing and unspoiled beaches, head for the western shore of Phuket. For Hollywood-style beauty and incredible nightlife, cruise to the world-famous Phi Phi islands, Phang Nga Bay and do some island hopping.

The sheltering coast protects the staggering beauty of protected Maya Bay, the location for the film 'The Beach,' while nearby Ko Lanta hides isolated villages and some of the best cuisine in Southeast Asia. A Phuket sailing yacht vacation will introduce you to a world of exotic beauty and idyllic islands. Be sure to choose Draco Charters!

DRACO CHARTERS

www.dracocharters.com

CREDITS

Author: Ben Lacey (Pen name Ben Sonimsart)

Copy editor: Amber Freeman - Proofing You Write

Sponsor: Draco Charters

Cover artist and formatter: Riyad Sapri

Food Chapter Feature: Gary Butler – The Roaming Cook (options 14 to 23)

Photos of food options 14 to 23: Gary Butlet – The Roaming Cook.

Front Cover Photo: Adisak_Nop /shutterstock.com

Printed in July 2019
by Rotomail Italia S.p.A., Vignate (MI) - Italy